Dennett

THE *ONEWORLD THINKERS* SERIES:

Each book in the *Oneworld Thinkers* series introduces the life and works of a major intellectual figure, exploring their most influential ideas and their lasting legacy. Accessibly written by prominent academics, the books in this series are a must-have for anyone interested in ideas.

Currently Available

Nietzsche
Robert Wicks
ISBN 1–85168–485–9

Wittgenstein
Avrum Stroll
ISBN 1–85168–486–7

Rawls
Paul Graham
ISBN 1–85168–483–2

Forthcoming

Aquinas
Edward Feser

Berkeley
Harry M. Bracken

Derrida
David Cunningham

Dewey
David Hildebrand

Eco
Florian Mussgnug

Habermas
David Ingram

Hobbes
Alistair Edwards

Hume
Harold Noonan

Huxley
Kieron O'Hara

Jung
Susan Rowland

Locke
Edward Feser

Dennett

Tadeusz Zawidzki

ONEWORLD THINKERS

ONEWORLD
OXFORD

DENNETT

Published by Oneworld Publications 2007

ISBN-13: 978–1–85168–484–7
ISBN-10: 1–85168–484–0

Typeset by Jayvee, Trivandrum, India
Cover design by Simon McFadden
Printed and bound by Bell & Bain Ltd., Glasgow

Oneworld Publications
185 Banbury Road
Oxford OX2 7AR
England
www.oneworld-publications.com

To Sophie Z., without whom this book would not be.
And to Katie Z., without whom Sophie Z. would not be.

Contents

CONTENTS

Preface

I came to this project with some standard assumptions about Dennett's work. I have been reading Dennett since deciding to major in philosophy as an undergraduate, and over the years I had come to accept the consensus evaluation of his work: although undeniably creative and important, it supposedly lacks philosophical depth and is not systematic. Consensus has it that Dennett's approach is diffuse and piecemeal, involving clever discussions of specific problems at the intersection of philosophy and the sciences of human nature, without the backing of an overarching, philosophical system. Many of Dennett's admirers, sceptical of the excesses of traditional philosophical systems, see this approach as a virtue (Rorty 1993, pp. 191–192; Ross 2000, pp. 16–23). Indeed, Dennett himself often blithely dismisses the importance of philosophical system-building (Ross 2000, p. 13; Dennett 2000, pp. 356, 359).

Writing this book has significantly changed my view of Dennett's work. If the reader comes away with anything from the following, I want it to be an appreciation of the fact that Dennett's work constitutes a deeply coherent philosophical system, founded on a few consistently applied principles. 'System' means different things to different people. To many philosophers, it means the systematic exploration of all logically possible distinctions relevant to traditionally important philosophical problems. It is undeniable that Dennett's corpus does *not* constitute a system in this sense. Dennett famously argues that many logically possible distinctions explored by the philosophical tradition are dead ends.[1] However, there is another sense of philosophical systems expressed by the American philosopher Wilfrid Sellars, an important influence on Dennett: 'The aim of philosophy,' he writes 'is to understand how things in the broadest possible sense of the term hang together in the broadest possible sense of the term' (Sellars 1963, p. 1). On this understanding of philosophical systems, Dennett's corpus constitutes a philosophical system, par excellence. Few philosophers have attempted to bring together, in one coherent framework, as broad a range of human inquiry as Dennett has.

There is another misapprehension of Dennett's work with which I do not deal explicitly in the following. Many complain that he does not address questions of value, like ethical and political issues. In a blog discussion of his most recent book, *Breaking the Spell: Religion as a Natural Phenomenon* (2006), one contributor goes so far as to describe Dennett's worldview as 'nihilistic'. It is true that there is little explicit discussion of questions of value in Dennett's corpus. However, reading between the lines, especially in his work on freedom of the will, it is impossible to escape the impression that Dennett is driven by a deep and passionate commitment to humanistic values: freedom, personal responsibility, rationality, knowledge and intellectual inquiry. According to Dennett, a scientific worldview is not, as some claim, at odds with such values. Quite the contrary: a proper appreciation of what science is discovering about our species shows that such values are central to human nature. Although I do not discuss this explicitly, I hope the reader comes away with a sense of Dennett's passionate commitment to core humanistic values.

This book has benefited enormously from the support and criticism of colleagues. Mark LeBar, James Petrik and Nathaniel Goldberg all read full drafts, making insightful criticisms that have undoubtedly improved the book. Any remaining deficiencies are entirely my fault. I also thank Andrew Brook for his role in making this book possible. E-mail correspondence with Daniel Dennett, during the writing of the first draft, was also of tremendous assistance. The comments of two anonymous reviewers engaged by Oneworld were also very helpful. Last, but definitely not least, I thank Don Ross. His insightful and thorough commentary on a draft of the final chapter is the least of his contributions. Don not only introduced me to Dennett's work; he convinced me to pursue a career in philosophy. In addition, I first heard the idea that Dennett's corpus has many features of a philosophical system from Don.[2] In fact, I think he is the only person I have ever heard interpret Dennett this way. After a thorough study of Dennett's corpus, I have come to agree with this minority view.

Besides the scholarly support I have received from colleagues, I have been sustained in this project by the love and encouragement of close friends and family. I especially want to thank my wife Kate Zawidzki, my daughter Sophia Zawidzki and my good friend Al Lent.

A note on the references

Key books by Dennett are referenced within the text by the following letter codes:

BS   *Brainstorms* (1978)
ER   *Elbow Room* (1984)
IS   *The Intentional Stance* (1987)
CE   *Consciousness Explained* (1991)
DDI   *Darwin's Dangerous Idea* (1995)
BC   *Brainchildren* (1998)
FE   *Freedom Evolves* (2003)
SD   *Sweet Dreams* (2005)

Chapter One

Dennett's project in context

Preamble

Daniel Clement Dennett is one of the most influential philosophers of mind of the past thirty years. His influence, like his interests and projects, transcends disciplinary boundaries: besides philosophy, his views are respected and engaged with in fields as disparate as artificial intelligence, cognitive psychology, neuroscience, evolutionary biology and anthropology. Dennett's forays into the scientific study of the mind are no accident; they are the inevitable development of the philosophical project that defines his career. This is arguably the dominant project of Western philosophy since the rise of modern science: reconciling our common-sense, traditional conception of ourselves with the scientific understanding of human nature.

The American philosopher Wilfrid Sellars captured the tension between these conceptions in particularly vivid language. According to Sellars, modern philosophy seeks to reconcile the 'manifest image' with the 'scientific image' of man (Sellars 1963, p. 6). The manifest image is the image that we all take for granted. Human beings are persons, with conscious thoughts and desires, freedom of the will and, consequently, responsibility for our actions. The scientific image appears as a jarring repudiation of these assumptions. Human beings are nothing but physical systems, composed of simple biochemical components arranged in dazzlingly complex, self-maintaining configurations, constructed from genetic blueprints selected for and passed down in evolution, under the influence of countless environmental variables. How can such systems have conscious thoughts and desires? How can such systems freely choose their actions in light of their conscious thoughts and desires? How can such systems be responsible for what they do?

A natural reaction to the seeming chasm between the manifest and scientific images of human nature is to reject either one or the other. Such rejections have been proposed since the earliest philosophical treatments of this problem. For example, Rêné Descartes, rightly considered the father of modern philosophy of mind for his explicit appreciation of the problem, rejected the application of the scientific image to the human mind. According to his theory of Cartesian Dualism, the mind is a non-physical, non-mechanical substance that interacts with the brain to cause behaviour. On the other hand, some contemporary philosophers, like Paul Churchland (1981) and Stephen Stich (1983), arrive at the opposite conclusion: rather than rejecting the scientific image of the human mind, they reject (parts of) the manifest image. Despite appearances, human beings are *not really* free agents, responsible for the actions that they choose in light of their conscious beliefs and desires.[1] Dennett, like Sellars, is concerned to avoid such extreme views. He respects science as the final word on human nature, yet he refuses to dismiss the manifest image. Our conception of ourselves as conscious thinkers and responsible, free agents is, according to Dennett, a fundamentally important fact about human nature. It cannot be dismissed. Somehow, both the scientific and the manifest images must be right. Fundamentally, Dennett's project, like Sellars', is a highly original and ingenious attempt to show how this can be; how it can be the case both (1) that human beings are conscious, thinking, free, responsible agents, and (2) that human beings are purely natural products of evolution, composed of simple biochemical components, arranged in complex, self-maintaining configurations.

In this chapter, I situate Dennett's approach in the context of the tradition he calls his own and compare it to competing approaches, but before I turn to this historical survey, I want to discuss, in more detail and with more precision, the problem that motivates Dennett and most other philosophers of mind since Descartes. What, precisely, are the key components of the manifest image of human nature and of the scientific image of human nature? And, why, precisely, are these two conceptions of human nature in conflict? Why can't a complex, self-maintaining config-uration of simple biochemical components, produced by natural selection, be a conscious, thinking, free, responsible agent?

The manifest image

Intentionality

Consider some of the capacities that we all take persons to have. First and foremost, persons can *think*. What does this mean? Thoughts are, nearly always, thoughts *about* something. Persons have thoughts about other persons, about their own bodies, about places they have been or would like to go, about foods they have eaten or would like to eat, about experiences they have had or would like to have, and even about other thoughts. So, a person's capacity to think is a capacity to think *about something*. Philoso-phers have a slightly confusing, technical term for this: 'intention-ality'. In everyday English, to do something intentionally is to do it on purpose. But 'intentionality', as philosophers understand it, has a different, though related meaning: it is the property of being about something. Thoughts have intentionality because they are about things. In other words, they *represent*, or are *directed at* other objects, events, or situations. Usually thoughts in a person's mind are directed at objects, events, or situations in the world outside their mind, but they can also be directed at other thoughts in their mind, such as when they think about opinions they used to hold but have long abandoned.

Thoughts are not the only things with intentionality. For example, words have intentionality. The word 'cat,' that is, the letter string C-A-T, is about, or stands for, cats, the fuzzy, temperamental mammals that many persons keep as pets. Many pictures also have intentionality. Van Gogh's self-portraits are directed at Van Gogh and a photograph of Christina Ricci represents Christina Ricci. But it is arguable that the intentionality of thoughts is the most import-ant kind of intentionality. Words and pictures get their intentional-ity from us. For example, the word 'cat' stands for cats because human beings invented the word to express thoughts about cats. And pictures of Christina Ricci represent Christina Ricci because they call to mind thoughts about Christina Ricci. This leads many philosophers to conclude that thoughts have 'original intentionality', while the intentionality of words, pictures and other human prod-ucts is merely 'derived' (IS, p. 288). Rejecting this distinction is cen-tral to Dennett's view, and I will return to it in subsequent chapters.

Not only are there many kinds of things with intentionality, there are also many kinds of thoughts. Let us call the object, or situation, or event that a thought is about the thought's *content*. Suppose you have a thought the content of which you take to be true. For example, you think there is a beer in the fridge and, after checking, you see that it is true that there is a beer in the fridge, so you take it to be true. To take something to be true is to *believe* it, so thoughts the contents of which persons take to be true are called *beliefs*. Suppose, on the other hand, that you have a thought the content of which you *want* to be true. For example, you think about drinking the beer, and you realize you want this to happen, so you want it to be true. To want something to be true is to *desire* it, so thoughts the contents of which persons want to be true are called *desires*.

There are also many other kinds of thoughts, like fears, hopes, worries, regrets, etc. All of these kinds of thoughts have intention-ality and therefore content: they are about objects or situations or events. The differences between these kinds of thoughts consist in different kinds of attitudes towards thought-content. Fearing that the world is on the brink of religious war involves an attitude of fear towards the content of one's thought, namely, the world's being on the brink of religious war; hoping that a religious war can be avoided involves an attitude of hope towards the content of one's thought, namely, a religious war being avoided; and so on for all the other kinds of thoughts. In light of this, it is natural to conceive of thoughts as attitudes towards contents, i.e. towards ways the world might be, as these are represented by the mind. Such contents are specified using sentences. For example, the content of my fear that the world is on the brink of religious war is specified using the sentence 'the world is on the brink of religious war'. Because the contents of thoughts are specified by sentences, many philosophers assume that thought-contents have a sentential or, to use a more technical term, *propositional* form. And because thoughts are naturally understood as attitudes towards such contents, philosophers call thoughts 'propositional attitudes'.

We often explain the actions of persons by appeal to their propositional attitudes. The most common kind of explanation alludes to a person's beliefs and desires. If I reach into the fridge, the best explanation for this might be that I believe that there is beer in the fridge and I desire that I drink beer. This common sense way of explaining human behaviour is sometimes called 'folk psychology' by philosophers. The idea is that, just as we are raised with a 'folksy' understanding of animals, plants, physical objects and other everyday domains, we are also raised with a 'folksy' understanding of what makes persons tick. According to this understanding, persons do what they do because of what they believe and desire. Another term used by philosophers for this way of explaining human behaviour is 'intentional psychology'. The reason for this should be obvious: when you explain someone's behaviour by appeal to their beliefs and desires, you are explaining it by appeal to states with intentionality, that is, thoughts that are *about* objects, or persons, or situations, etc. Yet another term for folk psychology is 'propositional attitude psychology'.

The final feature of persons' capacity to think, to which I want to draw attention, is that persons' thoughts are quite often mistaken. A person might believe that they have an appointment at 10 a.m., yet they may be mistaken; the appointment might be at 11 a.m. instead. More dramatically, persons often have all sorts of beliefs that cannot be true because they are about things that do not exist. Helen might believe that Frodo the hobbit is off fighting orcs with

Gandalf the wizard. The capacity to think about situations that do not and, indeed, *could* not transpire is a particularly puzzling feature of persons' capacity to think. I will return to this puzzling feature of thoughts later in this chapter, when I discuss attempts to reconcile the scientific and manifest images of human beings: it is one of the key obstacles to this project.

Consciousness

Consciousness is perhaps the most mysterious feature of persons as they are portrayed by the manifest image. Part of the reason for the mystery is that consciousness is very hard to define. One classic way of elucidating the concept of consciousness is in terms of the phrase 'what it is like to be'. The American philosopher Thomas Nagel coined this phrase in order to make a point about the limits of science (Nagel, 1974). Science tries to understand objects, including animals and persons, *objectively*, from the *outside*, from a *third-person perspective*. Nagel argues that no amount of such objective, external, third-person information about an animal (his example is a bat) could tell us what it is like to be the animal. There is something it is like to be a bat, yet this is only available to the bat: it is *subjective*, or *first-person* information. This subjective realm, forever beyond the reach of objective science, is, according to Nagel, the realm of consciousness.

We can gain a better understanding of the realm of consciousness by considering some classic philosophical puzzles. Try the following experiment. Run two taps of water, the first at a lukewarm temperature, the second at an ice-cold temperature. Put one hand in the stream of lukewarm water. Now put the same hand in the stream of ice-cold water. Finally, return the hand to the stream of lukewarm water. How does it feel? If you are like most people, the lukewarm water feels much hotter the second time around. But where is all this extra, felt heat? The temperature of the lukewarm water has stayed constant, so it cannot be in the water. It must be inside you. Yet, no matter how much I study your skin, or your nerves, or your brain from the outside, in a scientific, objective way, I cannot find the extra heat. All I see are skin cells and nerve cells firing. I never find the feeling of the water being hotter. So where is it? In the realm of consciousness. Here is another example. Come up as close to a building as possible so that you can still see the entire structure at once. Now start moving away from the building slowly. The building should appear to shrink. But where is this shrinking building? It is not out in the world. The actual building is not shrinking; it remains the same size. So, is the shrinking building inside you? Is it some kind of visual image? If it is, then it cannot be studied scientifically or objectively, for, if I look inside your eye, or in your brain, all I see are nerve cells firing; I do not see a shrinking image of the building. The shrinking image of the building, like the extra, felt heat of the water, is in the realm of consciousness.

Philosophers generally distinguish between two kinds of consciousness. First, there is the kind of consciousness that humans share with many other species of animal. Humans and many animals experience sensations like pain, pleasure, hunger, fear, etc. These are conscious states: it is hard to see how studying human beings or animals from the outside could ever reveal what it is like for a human being or animal to experience such sensations. The second kind of consciousness is restricted to human beings and, perhaps, our nearest primate cousins, chimpanzees. This kind of consciousness is often called 'self-consciousness'. Though it is plausible that many animals have experiences, it is doubtful that most animals *conceive of themselves* as having experiences. Compare feeling pain with conceiving of yourself as feeling pain. It is hard to deny that animals and young infants can experience pain, but it is also hard to believe that when they experience pain they think of themselves as experiencing pain.

According to the manifest image of persons, persons are not only conscious, they are self-conscious. In addition, persons are considered experts about what they are conscious of at a particular time. If a person sincerely reports that she is in pain, then she must be in pain. Descartes, again, articulates the classic version of this assumption. He claims that a person's mind is utterly transparent to the person: the person cannot be mistaken about what they are conscious of, nor can they be conscious of something without knowing it (Descartes 1984, p. 19). This view is one of Dennett's major targets: he calls it the doctrine of the 'Cartesian Theatre'. The idea is that a person becomes conscious of an experience, or feeling, or thought when it appears on a metaphorical 'stage' in the mind, on display for the person's self. Introspection is understood as a kind of inward gaze: persons look inside their minds to see what they are thinking and experiencing.

According to the manifest image, persons' conscious experiences are also taken to be *ineffable*. This means that there is no way of conveying the precise nature of a conscious experience using public language; words cannot describe what it is like for a person to experience what they are experiencing. Imagine explaining what the colour red looks like to a blind person.

Most people do not make a clear distinction between thought and consciousness. Yet here, and in Dennett's work, and in philosophy of mind in general, the propositional attitudes and consciousness are generally treated separately. There are several reasons for this. Foremost is the fact that conscious experiences are taken to be ineffable. It is very difficult, if not impossible, to convey the precise nature of conscious experiences using public language. Yet the contents of propositional attitudes are always specified in terms of public language sentences. So consciousness and thought differ in one important respect: while the latter is easily expressible in language, the former is not.

Another reason for distinguishing between thought and consciousness is the possibility of unconscious thoughts. Since Sigmund Freud first proposed that human behaviour can often be explained in terms of unconscious beliefs and desires, many philosophers and psychologists have accepted the possibility that some of our thoughts are unconscious. This suggests that what makes something a thought is very different from what makes something a conscious state. On reflection, it seems clear that persons have a lot of beliefs about the world of which they are not explicitly aware. As you read this, you probably believe that there are no live whales within three inches of you, but prior to reading this, you were not conscious of this belief. So, it seems plausible that you can have beliefs, and other propositional attitudes, without being conscious of them.

Although consciousness and thought tend to be treated separately by philosophers of mind, including Dennett, there are clearly connections between consciousness and thought. Many of our thoughts are conscious, and perhaps all of them are at least potentially conscious. Furthermore, according to the manifest image of persons, conscious thought is the normal, primary case. Unconscious thoughts, if they exist, are exceptions. All thoughts are always poised to come out onto the 'stage' of the 'Cartesian Theatre' for a person's 'inner eye' to observe. And the 'inner eye' cannot be wrong about the contents of the thoughts it examines: it always knows exactly how such thoughts represent the world; it always knows exactly what the person is thinking about.

Given that thought and consciousness, though distinct, are intimately related, it is interesting to investigate *how* they are related. The philosophical tradition inaugurated by Descartes sees consciousness as primary. If we want to know what thought is, and what thoughts a person is thinking, we must first explain what consciousness and, especially, self-consciousness are. Once we know this, we can examine the contents of consciousness, the 'actors' on the 'stage' of the Cartesian Theatre, to discover what thoughts are, and which thoughts a particular person is thinking. Unconscious thoughts, if there are such, can then be treated as a derivative case. One of Dennett's central claims is the explicit repudiation of this Cartesian strategy. Dennett's entire project begins by reversing the traditional priority of consciousness over thought. He tries to understand what thought is, and what it is to have a particular thought, independently of understanding consciousness. He then tries to explain consciousness and self-consciousness, as special kinds of thought. According to Dennett, this is crucial to the project of reconciling the manifest and the scientific images of persons.

Since science traffics in objective, third-person information, any strategy for understanding thought and mind that begins with consciousness, which is supposedly a realm of first-person, subjective information, puts thought and mind beyond the reach of science. Dennett begins by trying to understand thought in third-person, objective terms that are amenable to scientific study. He then tries to understand consciousness, subjectivity and the first-person perspective as a kind of thought, ultimately also amenable to scientific study. This strategy is fundamental to understanding Dennett's entire philosophical project, and I return to it repeatedly in subsequent chapters.

Self and agency

There are two more important features of the manifest image of persons. First is the notion of the self. According to the manifest image, within a person's mind resides a kind of 'central executive' that is in charge of the whole operation. This is the 'inner eye' that observes the unfolding drama in the Cartesian Theatre. Besides being the inner eye, the central executive is also the ultimate source of control: it issues commands that determine what the person does next. The senses deliver information about the outside world to the self. Information about bodily needs is also provided. The self then determines how best to fulfil these needs given the state of the outside world. The self is rather like the captain of a ship or the general of an army. It is supposed to be a single 'place' in the mind where all information relevant to deciding what to do next comes together, and where the decision about what to do next is made.

The manifest image of persons also includes a very specific notion of what it is to be an agent that is closely related to this conception of the self. To understand what an agent is, one must first understand the distinction between actions and mere motions. Human bodies are often in motion, but not all of these motions are considered actions. Nervous twitches, reflex behaviour like kicking in response to a tap under the kneecap, slips of the tongue, and unintended jerks are all motions that human bodies undergo, but they are not considered actions. What is the difference between such motions and motions that we call 'actions'? An obvious answer is that actions are motions done deliberately, on purpose, or intentionally (in the standard, non-philosophical sense of this term). But what makes a motion deliberate, or purposeful, or intentional? According to the manifest image, human behaviour is deliberate if it is the result of a process of deliberation. Behaviour that is caused by a decision to act, that is the result of reasoning about the best way to achieve some purpose in light of certain information about the world, qualifies as action. For example, my raising my arm to open the fridge, if it is the result of a decision arrived at through reasoning about the best way to achieve some goal, like drinking beer, in light of certain information about the world, like the presence of beer in the fridge, counts as an action. If the raising of my arm is the result of a nervous twitch, then it is not an action.

Given this understanding of action, it is easy to explain what agents are. Agents are systems, for example human beings, capable of controlling their behaviour by deciding what to do on the basis of reasoning about how best to achieve goals given certain information about the world. Given the understanding of the self as a central executive that makes such decisions, it seems clear that, according to the manifest image of persons, agents are bodies with 'selves' controlling them.

These notions of self and agency are fundamental to the manifest image of persons. They underlie one of the key properties of persons. Persons, more than anything else, are objects that can be held *responsible* for what they do. When a person does something wrong, like stealing another person's money, they should be punished. When a person does something right, like inventing a useful gadget, they should be rewarded. The assumption appears to be that, when a person decides to do something, they do it freely and so are responsible for what they decide to do. Persons are not normally held responsible for behaviour over which they have no control, i.e., for behaviour that is not the result of any decision on their part. If a person accidentally takes someone's money, believing it to be their own, then they are not held responsible. This is because the action of taking another's money is not deliberate: not knowing that the money is not their own, the person does not decide to take someone else's money. Thus, the notion that persons are agents controlled by selves, free to decide how to act, in the light of the information they have available, underlies some of our most fundamental and cherished ideals and institutions. The possibility of holding persons responsible for their actions, on which ideals like justice and virtue, and institutions like the law depend, appears to presuppose that persons are free agents, controlled by selves that are ultimately responsible for reasoning to decisions about how to act.

The scientific image

Neuroscience

The sciences of the human nervous system, the neurosciences, are currently in a very early stage of development. There is nothing approaching the consensus that characterizes mature sciences like physics, chemistry and biology. Though data gathered about the human nervous system is voluminous and growing exponentially, there is very little theoretical insight about the significance of this data. Nobody claims to *know* how what we know about the nervous system explains the operation of the nervous system, and its role in human behaviour. Nevertheless, there are some basic facts about the nervous system that are beyond dispute, and despite their early stage of development, the neurosciences are already constructing an image of human nature that is very unlike the manifest image.

The sciences of human nature, including neuroscience, biology and cognitive science, assume that human behaviour is entirely a product of the nervous system. If this assumption turns out correct in any sense, then a 'showdown' with the manifest image of persons appears inevitable. Nervous systems are composed entirely of physical components: cells and tissues constructed out of proteins, communicating using chemical and electrical signals. The consensus in human biology is that nervous systems, like other biological systems, are products of evolution by natural selection. Current humans have the nervous systems they have because we are descended from a long line of 'lucky mutants'. Each of our evolutionary ancestors was better at surviving and reproducing than countless other creatures because of a lucky quirk, a difference in how they were built, and thus in how they behaved. Over time, these lucky quirks added up, and among the most important products of this process are current human nervous systems: repositories of biological quirks that have proven useful in controlling behaviour, in a way that promotes the survival and transmission of the genes that code for them. This is a minimal understanding of the human nervous system with which the over-whelming majority of scientists studying human nature agree. Yet even this minimal conception is already in dramatic tension with the manifest image of persons.

Intentionality and the brain

Consider the property of intentionality, which, according to the manifest image, is a crucial feature of thoughts that persons have. To say that a thought has intentionality is to say that it is directed at an object or a situation; it is to say that the thought represents the world as being a certain way. According to the manifest image, much of our behaviour is caused by thoughts, specifically by beliefs and desires. But, according to the consensus in the sciences of human nature, all human behaviour is ultimately caused by states of the nervous system and, especially, the brain. Suppose then that we look at some state of the brain, say a pattern of activation across a popu-lation of nerve cells that we know causes certain behaviours. How can we tell whether this pattern of neural activation is a thought, and which thought it is? How can we tell what this pattern of neural activation is about, what situation or object in the world it is directed at, or represents? In itself, the pattern of neural activation is nothing but a kind of chemical or electrical activity among a set of biological structures. What makes this pattern into a representation of some situation? What makes it *mean* what it does, if anything?

This is similar to a question we can ask about words. In itself, the word 'cat' is just a bunch of geometric shapes and lines. There is nothing about it, in itself, that explains why it means what it does, why it stands for cats. If you have difficulty understanding this problem, try repeating some word, like 'cat', many times in a row, very quickly. Upon doing this, many people notice how strange an ordinary word, like 'cat', begins to sound. One starts to wonder why the word for cat must sound like *that*; one notices a disconnection between how the word sounds and what the word *means*. This experience is a kind of realization that nothing about words in themselves, their shape, sound, or appearance, explains why they mean what they do. In the case of words, we can explain what they mean by appeal to the intentions of language users. English speakers intend to use the word 'cat' to stand for cats, and that is why 'cat' stands for cats. Such an explanation is unavailable in the case of patterns of neural activity. There are no persons in the brain deciding to use patterns of neural activity to stand for cats or anything else. So the question remains, if thoughts about cats, say, are nothing but patterns of neural activity, then what makes these patterns of neural activity stand for, or represent, something as different from them as cats?

The human capacity to think about objects that do not exist in physical space and time constitutes another obstacle to reconciling the scientific image of human nature with the commonsense assumption that thoughts have intentionality. Brain states exist in real space and time. They have a definite location and duration. So they can only be related to other events and objects that exist in space and time. For example, they can be triggered by light that reflects off real objects, hits the retina in the eye, and is consequently transduced into neural impulses in the brain. But human beings can think about things that do not exist in space and time. Human thoughts can be directed at numbers and other abstract mathematical objects. Humans can think about abstract ideals like justice and beauty. Furthermore, human beings often think about things that do not exist in any sense. Above, I gave the example of Helen, who believes that Frodo the hobbit is off fighting orcs with Gandalf the wizard. But Frodo, hobbits, orcs, Gandalf and wizards do not exist *at all*, let alone in space and time. If science is right and all human behaviour is caused by states of the nervous system, then it appears that the only way the manifest image of persons can be maintained is if thoughts are states of the nervous system. But how can a state of the nervous system, a pattern of neural activation, existing in space and time, be about or directed at objects that do not exist in space and time? To be about something, or to represent something, or to be directed at something, is to be related to it. If brain states are purely physical, then it is hard to see how they can be related in any way to things that do not exist in physical space and time, so it is hard to see how brain states could be thoughts about numbers, or other abstract objects, or fictional entities. Since the capacity to think such thoughts is an important part of the manifest image of persons, this constitutes another obstacle to reconciling the manifest image with the scientific image of human nature.

Consciousness and the brain

I have already discussed some of the ways in which consciousness, as portrayed in the manifest image of persons, conflicts with the scientific understanding of human beings. On the standard view, consciousness is what it is like to be a person. This kind of information is essentially subjective. No amount of objective information can reveal what it is like to be someone. But everything that science discovers about the brain is objective information: it is available from the third-person; anyone can access it. Yet, for some philosophers, consciousness is defined as precisely that which cannot be captured in such objective terms. So it seems inevitable that consciousness cannot be reconciled with the scientific image of human nature.

Even if we reject such a definition of consciousness as unfairly prejudging the issue of whether consciousness can be studied scientifically, there remain obvious obstacles to reconciling the scientific image of human nature as determined by the nervous system with the manifest image of persons as conscious entities. Recall that consciousness seems to represent the world in a way that is very unlike the way the world is. Structures appear to shrink as we move away from them. Water appears to change temperature even when we know it has not. So the way the world is cannot be confused with the way the world appears in consciousness: but then, where is this world of appearances? When we look inside a person's brain, we do not find the way the world appears to the person. We do not find shrinking buildings, or water that changes temperature for no objective reason. All we find are patterns of neural activity. Smells, tastes, sensations, images cannot be in external objects because they can change even while objects stay the same. So, according to the manifest image, they must be within the person experiencing them; but if we look inside the person, by examining her nervous system using the tools of neuroscience, we do not find smells, tastes, sensations, or images. We just find patterns of neural activity. Again, the scientific image of human nature seems at odds with the manifest image of persons.

In general, the world of appearances, presented in consciousness, seems very different from the world of the brain, revealed by science. The world of appearances contains objects with properties. For example, consider seeing, touching, picking up and biting into a green apple. The colour, weight, texture, smell and taste of the apple all seem bound together in one object. In consciousness, the apple appears as a unified object, but when we look in the brain, we see that neural states coding for these different kinds of information are widely distributed. One part of the brain is responsible for detecting colour, another for judging weight, a third for detecting texture, a fourth for processing smell, a fifth for detecting taste. How do all of these disparate kinds of information get bound together in the representation of one object, the apple? Cognitive scientists call this the 'binding problem' (Hardcastle 1998). Another difference between the world of appearance and the world of the brain involves the contrast between the smoothness of the former and the 'choppiness' of the latter. The world usually appears to persons as a smooth, continuous, stable flow of events, which some have termed 'the stream of consciousness', but brain activity is not like this at all. During a single, seemingly uninterrupted, continuous experience, different parts of the brain are rapidly turning on and off. How can the smooth, stable, continuous stream of consciousness emerge from such a flurry of apparently chaotic, disconnected activity?

Finally, recall the Cartesian Theatre. According to the manifest image, thoughts and sensations appear on a metaphorical stage to be examined by an inner eye, but there does not appear to be any place in the brain where this happens. Information is widely distributed in the brain, and there is no place where it all comes together on some 'stage' or 'monitor' for the self to examine. This is a version of the problem discussed above concerning intentionality. Though you can explain the intentionality of words like 'cat' in terms of a decision by speakers to use 'cat' to stand for cats, this explanation does not work for brain states. There are no people inside brains that decide that some pattern of neural activity stands for cats. In the same way, there are no people inside brains observing some stage or monitor where all the information processed by the brain comes together. Both of these ideas are versions of a mistake that cognitive scientists seek, not always successfully, to avoid: the homunculus fallacy. A homunculus is a little person. If you are trying to explain how persons are capable of performing certain tasks, you cannot appeal to little persons hidden in their brains that are capable of performing the same tasks. Any such appeal cannot be an explanation, because it raises the same questions over again for the homunculi. The idea that a human person is visually conscious of objects in front of them because a homunculus inside them is visually conscious of these objects projected onto something like a monitor in the brain, besides being obviously false, is not even an explanation, because it explains the consciousness of one person in terms of the consciousness of another. This is a favourite point of Dennett's to which I will return in subsequent chapters.

The point to remember here is that brains do not have homunculi inside them[2] and, even if they did, this could not explain how persons think. This is a problem because, according to the manifest image of persons, consciousness seems like the Cartesian Theatre: it seems like a place where all of our thoughts and sensations come together for the self to examine. If there is no such place in the nervous system, then the scientific image of human nature is, once again, in conflict with the manifest image of persons.

Agency and the brain

The final obstacle to reconciling the manifest image with the scientific image of human nature concerns our pre-scientific notions of agency. It should already be apparent, from the foregoing discussion of the homunculus fallacy, that the notion of the self as a central executive that calls all the shots in the mind is at odds with the picture of the nervous system emerging from neuroscience. There does not appear to be a central location in the brain that has access to all the information, and that uses this information to come to decisions about what to do next. In many respects, the brain is more like a 'society' of control systems, sometimes cooperating, sometimes competing for control of an individual's overall behaviour (Minsky 1985; CE). The notion that there is someone in charge in there, responsible for coming to rational decisions, based on a careful consideration of all available information, appears to be an illusion. This scientific understanding of the nervous system appears to have drastic implications for our everyday notions of agency, freedom and responsibility.

If all human behaviour is ultimately caused by the nervous system, and if the nervous system is nothing but a loosely organized conspiracy of quasi-independent control systems, sometimes cooperating, sometimes competing for control of behaviour, then it is hard to see how persons can be free to behave as they do, and how persons can be held responsible for what they do. This worry becomes even more pressing when one realizes that this conspiracy of control systems that constitutes the brain is composed of relatively simple biochemical components, namely, cells, arranged in complex, self-maintaining configurations, constructed from genetic information passed down over the course of evolution. To borrow an image from the biologist Richard Dawkins, an important influence on Dennett's thinking, we are nothing but elaborate survival machines, robots constructed by our genes as a way of surviving and being passed on (Dawkins 1976). How can such mechanisms, no matter how complex, be free to act as they want?

According to the scientific image, we have been 'designed' by natural selection to pass on genes. Everything we do, when functioning properly, is driven by this goal. Even when we malfunction, what we do is caused by our malfunctioning, biochemical parts. But how can anything constructed out of entirely biochemical parts be free? Such parts are physical, and physical things must follow the laws of physics. Anything composed of such parts is likewise physical and must follow the laws of physics, whether it wants to or not. So if persons are elaborate survival machines, composed of purely physical parts bound by the laws of physics, as science appears to show, then how can persons be free? And if they cannot be free, then how can they be responsible for what they do? It seems that the scientific image really does throw the manifest image into jeopardy.

It is clear from this brief overview that the scientific and manifest images of human nature appear to be in serious tension with each other. Though still in their infancy, the sciences of human nature are constructing a picture of human nature that appears incompatible with our most cherished assumptions about what human persons are. If human behaviour is entirely determined by the human nervous system, then, on the face of it, it looks as though human beings cannot be the free, responsible, conscious, thinking, unified persons that the manifest image takes them to be.

Dennett's forty-year intellectual odyssey is an ambitious and ingenious attempt to resist this claim. He thinks that human beings are everything that science says they are. However, he argues that this is entirely compatible with their being free, responsible, conscious, thinking and unified persons, in any sense of these terms that is worth keeping. In the final section of this chapter, I situate Dennett's views in the context of other historically important attempts to grapple with the apparent chasm separating the scientific and the manifest images of human nature.

Dennett in historical context

Dualism and eliminativism

Let us call the problem of reconciling the scientific and manifest images the 'reconciliation problem'. I have already mentioned two historically important philosophical approaches to the reconciliation problem. Both of these approaches suggest that the problem cannot be solved: the scientific and manifest images cannot be reconciled. In the seventeenth century, the father of modern philosophy, Rêné Descartes, argued that the scientific image cannot be applied to the mind. We have seen that the mind, as portrayed in the manifest image, seems radically different from the nervous system, or indeed any physical system. Descartes concluded from this that the mind must not be a physical system. On his view, persons are composed of two substances: a physical substance (the body and its organs) and a non-physical, mental substance (the mind). For this reason, the view is called 'Cartesian *Dualism*'. Although this view is most closely associated with Descartes, there has been something of a contemporary revival. For example, the Australian philosopher David Chalmers has recently argued, in an influential book, that consciousness cannot be a physical property of the brain (Chalmers 1996).

Some contemporary philosophers advocate the other extreme. They agree with Descartes that the reconciliation problem cannot be solved, but instead of rejecting the application of the scientific image to the mind, they reject the manifest image. Despite appearances, human beings are not really conscious, thinking, free, responsible agents. This view is called 'eliminativism', because it advocates the elimination of the manifest image. Very few eliminativists advocate the elimination of every part of the manifest image. For example, the most influential contemporary eliminativist, Paul Churchland, advocates eliminating the propositional attitudes, yet he thinks that consciousness can be reconciled with what science has discovered about the nervous system.

There are good reasons to resist both extremes. Dualism is implausible for several reasons. One is the causal closure of the physical universe. It is a fundamental assumption of contemporary science that every physical event, everything that happens in the physical world, has a physical cause. In addition, there is no doubt that much human behaviour consists of physical events, e.g., the motion of a limb. It follows that if the mind is not physical then either states of mind do not cause human behaviour, or human behaviour is causally over-determined. The view that states of mind do not cause human behaviour is called 'epiphenomenalism'. Epiphenomenalism is very implausible: surely our emotions, thoughts and sensations cause us to do things. The alternative is that human behaviour often has two sets of causes: physical/neural causes and parallel non-physical/mental causes. But this kind of causal over-determination is very puzzling. What work is left for the mind to do if everything a human body does can be explained in terms of physical/neural causes?[3]

Eliminativism is no less implausible. On the face of it, it simply seems obvious that human beings are conscious, thinking, free, responsible agents. These are fundamental assumptions on which the most important human institutions depend. Indeed, it is hard to see how to understand *science itself* without assuming that scientists are conscious, thinking, free, responsible agents. When a scientist defends a theory, are they not expressing and defending something they *think* is true? Are they not responsible for the theory, and the arguments they construct in its favour? One common complaint about eliminativism is that it cannot be expressed and defended without presupposing what it denies. If someone claims that humans do not really have thoughts, is it not the case that they *think* that humans do not really have thoughts? Eliminativism does not just undermine fundamental assumptions on which the most important human institutions depend; it risks undermining *itself* as well![4]

Reductionism

The most influential contemporary approaches to the reconciliation problem attempt to avoid the problems associated with the extremes of dualism and eliminativism. Philosophy of mind in the twentieth century saw the emergence of two competing strategies for solving the reconciliation problem. The more influential strategy advocates *reductionism*. To paraphrase one of the foremost contemporary reductionists, for the mind to be real, it must be really something else (Fodor 1987, p. 97). Reductionism is inspired by successful theoretical identifications in the history of science. A successful theoretical identification occurs when a property referred to in an older, more limited theory is shown to be identical to a property referred to in a newer, more powerful theory. For example, chemistry has shown that the property of being water is nothing more than the property of being a substance composed of H_2O molecules. The scientific study of electromagnetism has shown that the property of being a flash of lightning is nothing more than the property of being an electrical discharge. The history of science is replete with such theoretical identifications, and they are taken, by reductionists, to be a sign of scientific progress. On this view, science is gradually showing that all phenomena are nothing more than physical phenomena. Reductionist philosophers of mind hope that the same fate awaits the mind as portrayed by the manifest image. Science will establish that the property of being a conscious, thinking, free, responsible agent is nothing more than some complex physical property, probably of the nervous system.

The twentieth century saw many different kinds of reductionism, some more plausible than others. The first wave of reductionism emerged in the 1950s. Philosophers such as Ullin T. Place, J. J. C. Smart and David Armstrong argued that properties attributed to the mind by the manifest image could be reduced to neural properties. For example, they argued that the property of being in pain might be identical with the property of some nerve fibres firing. Given the incompatibilities between the scientific and manifest images of human beings discussed above, it is unsurprising that this kind of reductionism did not catch on. We have seen that the realm of consciousness seems very different from the world of the brain, as science understands it. Patterns of neural activity do not seem like conscious experiences at all.

Neural reductionists tried to deflect such criticisms by pointing out an analogy to cases of successful reduction in the history of science. Water does not seem like a collection of H_2O molecules, but it is. Conscious experiences do not seem like patterns of neural activity, but perhaps they are nevertheless. Unfortunately, this sort of response has a fatal flaw. 'Seeming' presupposes an observer. Water seems not to be a collection of H_2O molecules *to us*, human observers. When we try to explain why conscious experiences do not seem like patterns of neural activity however, who is the observer? To whom do conscious experiences not seem like patterns of neural activity? If the reductionist says that this is not how they *appear* to us, she admits that there is a realm of appearance distinct from patterns of neural activity, but the realm of appearance just is the realm of conscious experience, precisely what the reductionist claims to be reducing to patterns of neural activity!

Another problem with this early, neural form of reductionism is the possibility that mental properties are *multiply realizable*. In the late 1950s and early 1960s, philosophers such as Hilary Putnam (1960) argued that mental properties, like the property of being in pain, could be exhibited, in principle, by systems composed of very different materials. For example, they argued that future robots, made of silicon and wire, or aliens made of unknown substances, or octopi, whose brains are very different from human brains, might all be able to feel pain. It follows that there is no reason to suppose that all systems capable of feeling pain have something physical in common. Though they may all be made of physical stuff, they may all be made of different physical stuff. This is what it means for a mental property, like being in pain, to be multiply realizable. Such multiple realizability rules out the neural reductionism discussed above. If, for example, the property of being in pain is multiply realizable, then it cannot be identified with the property of some nerve fibres firing, for systems without nerve fibres might feel pain.

At the time that he first proposed these arguments, Putnam urged that we replace the early, neural form of reductionism with a more sophisticated variety. Rather than reducing mental properties to neural properties, he urged that we reduce them to multiply realizable, functional or computational properties. He argued that cognitive systems, like the brain, can be modelled as computers. Just as computers can be understood as physical hardware running multiply realizable programming, or software, brains could be understood as physical 'wetware' running multiply realizable mental functions.[5] So, he advocated identifying mental properties, like being in pain, with computational or functional properties, like being in a state the function of which is to trigger avoidance behaviour in response to noxious stimuli.

The kind of reductionism proposed by Putnam, and defended by philosophers like Jerry Fodor (1975), is known as *functionalism*. Functionalism was the received solution to the reconciliation problem in late-twentieth century philosophy of mind. The computer model of the human mind still wields a powerful influence. Dennett himself, though no reductionist, sees computational models of human cognition as key to solving the reconciliation problem. Unfortunately, there is increasing consensus that functionalism is inadequate. Even Putnam, one of its earliest and ablest defenders, has abandoned it.

On reflection, it is unclear how functionalism makes any headway towards solving the problems of intentionality, consciousness and free will. The idea that mental states are identical to bits of software running on the brain, which is like a computer, sounds promising, until we realize that computers are neither free, nor conscious, nor do their internal states stand for anything other than what persons take them to stand for. Computers behave as their programs make them behave; they have no choice in the matter. And there is no reason to suppose there is anything it is like to be a computer. Even if there were, how would understanding the software running on a computer reveal what it is like to be the computer? Finally, though computer programs consist of symbols that appear to stand for objects and properties, for example, a value entered in a spreadsheet program might stand for a student's grade on a test, this is clearly a case of what, above, I called 'derived intentionality': symbols in computers stand for what their users and designers take them to stand for. But the intentionality of human thought does not seem to depend, in this way, on the intentions of users or designers.

The upshot of this brief discussion of reductionism as a strategy for solving the reconciliation problem is that, despite its promise and influence, it fails. The idea that if the mind is real, it must be really something else, fails as an attempt to reconcile the manifest and scientific images of human nature. Though computer programs are a suggestive metaphor for the mind, *identifying* mental properties with computational properties does not work for the same reason that identifying mental properties with neural properties does not work. The mental properties of the manifest image are just too different from neural and computational properties. This does not mean that studying the nervous system and constructing computational models are of no philosophical interest. As we shall see, for Dennett, they are indispensable to reconciling the scientific with the manifest image. However, there are different kinds of reconciliation. Reconciliation does not require *reducing* mental properties to, or *identifying* mental properties with neural or computational properties. The rest of this book is a detailed examination of Dennett's alternative form of reconciliation.

Dennett's tradition: logical behaviourism

The second prominent twentieth-century strategy for solving the reconciliation problem is more subtle than reductionism, and many of its defenders reject common labels for it as misleading. For convenience, I settle on the label 'logical behaviourism', but many representatives of this tradition would not accept this label. Logical behaviourists argue that the reconciliation problem is something of a pseudo-problem. The idea that there is a reconciliation problem, that the scientific and manifest images are in competition, rests on a kind of logical mistake. Once we understand the logic of the manifest image, the logic of the language we use to talk about consciousness, thought, responsibility, minds and persons, we see that it is entirely compatible with the language of the scientific image. Dennett is the foremost contemporary representative of this tradition. But he is also a maverick within this tradition.

Many of the most influential representatives of logical behaviourism, whose influence Dennett cheerfully acknowledges, like Ludwig Wittgenstein and Dennett's teacher, Gilbert Ryle, were dismissive of the scientific study of human nature. They did not see the relevance of the sciences of human nature to questions about the mind. To a rough approximation, traditional logical behaviourists interpret our common-sense language about consciousness, thought, responsibility, minds and persons as talk about observable patterns of behaviour. For example, to say that a person is in pain is *not* to make a claim about what is going on in some unobservable realm within her, to which only she has access. Rather, it is to claim that the person has a disposition to engage in a pattern of publicly observable behaviour, for example, wincing, groaning, complaining and seeking to remove the pain's source. Descartes' idea that thought, consciousness and will reside in a mysterious, unobservable realm within persons is a misguided metaphor that fails to capture what ordinary persons mean by words like 'thought', 'consciousness' and 'will'. Ryle lampoons this Cartesian metaphor as the myth of the 'ghost in the machine' (Ryle 1949). According to logical behaviourists, one could think that neuroscience or psychology are relevant to the philosophical study of the mind only if one were in the grip of this Cartesian myth. The myth leads one to expect that the scientific study of persons' innards, and especially their brains, will reveal their conscious minds, containing their true, heretofore concealed, thoughts and wishes. But this is at odds with the logical behaviourist analysis of our language about the mind. On this understanding, there are no hidden mental states waiting to be discovered within persons. The mental is on display, for all to see, in patterns of publicly observable behaviour.

Though Dennett is sympathetic with the lessons of logical behaviourism, he disagrees with their dismissal of science as irrelevant to philosophy of mind. Like another of his teachers, the influential American philosopher Willard Van Orman Quine, Dennett sees the work of philosophy as continuous with the work of science. This welcoming attitude towards science, the view that scientific discoveries about human beings are relevant to philosophical discussions of human persons, is called 'philosophical naturalism'.

Reductionists are diehard naturalists. They claim that the mind of the manifest image, the mind about which generations of philosophers have speculated, is nothing more than a set of properties of the nervous system, amenable to scientific study. Dennett is in a more difficult position. He comes from a philosophical tradition that denies the relevance of science to understanding the mind of the manifest image, yet he wants to integrate the insights of this tradition with the insights of the sciences of human nature. Not only does he want to do this; he argues that this approach is the only way of reconciling the scientific with the manifest image of human nature.

Basically, Dennett's strategy for solving the reconciliation problem is two-pronged. First, he wants to disabuse us of certain ways of thinking about the manifest image of persons. Part of the reason there seems to be a conflict between the manifest and scientific images is that the manifest image portrays the mind as a miraculous phenomenon. The mind consists of a self that has immediate and incorrigible access to any thought or experience within the mind. This self can use this information to come to lightning-quick, rational decisions about what to do next, and has absolute control over the behaviour of the body. These decisions are completely free; they are not constrained by the laws of nature. The mind is also full of appearances – shrinking buildings and water that turns hot for no objective reason, for example – that seem very different from real-world objects and properties. Yet this world of appearances is accessible to only one person: the person in whose mind they reside. They cannot be detected by anyone else: when others probe the person's insides they just find patterns of neural activity, no appearances. Finally, states of mind are somehow, magically, about things outside the mind and, indeed, about things that do not even exist in real space and time. Dennett's logical behaviourist precursors engaged in brilliant attempts to disabuse us of this image of the mind as a miraculous realm. Rather than being about some mysterious ghost in the machine, talk of the mind is about patterns of observable behaviour. Dennett assimilates this strategy: part of his goal is to *deflate* exotic, miracle-invoking accounts of the manifest image of the mind. The less miraculous the manifest image takes persons to be, the easier it is to reconcile it with the scientific image of human beings.

The second prong of Dennett's strategy consists in *inflating* the scientific image of human beings. Philosophers tend to denigrate the capacities of 'merely' physical systems studied by science. They tend to assume that physical systems can all be understood on antiquated, clockwork models of physical mechanisms. Even contemporary philosophers appear to have their imaginations captured by this seventeenth-century understanding of physical mechanisms. The great German philosopher of that era, Gottfried Wilhelm Leibniz, imagined being reduced in size so that he could examine the mechanisms of the brain, first-hand (Leibniz 1989, p. 215). He imagined exploring an immense clockwork mechanism of gears, pulleys and levers. He wondered: where in such a mechanism could one find consciousness? Unfortunately, as far as Dennett is concerned, the philosophical imagination has not progressed much since Leibniz's day. Dennett's close study of contemporary scientific models of the human mind–brain is aimed at rectifying this failure of imagination. He thinks that if we appreciate the wonderful, intricate complexity that science is uncovering in physical nature, it will be much easier to imagine how a purely physical system could nonetheless be a conscious, thinking, free, responsible agent.

Thus, Dennett's integration of two philosophical traditions that have sometimes seemed in conflict, logical behaviourism and philosophical naturalism, is essential to his goal of reconciling the scientific and manifest images of human nature. Logical behaviourism gives us tools to deflate the manifest image of persons: if we attend carefully to the logic of our talk about the mind, we see that it is not nearly as miraculous a realm as we have thought. Philosophical naturalism gives us tools to appreciate the wonder and complexity of nature: if we attend carefully to contemporary neuroscience, cognitive science, artificial intelligence and biology, we see that nature is not nearly as stupid as we have thought. Thus, although Dennett's logical behaviourism and philosophical naturalism seem, from the perspective of the history of philosophy, to be strange bedfellows, their alliance is actually extremely effective at showing that the scientific and manifest images of human nature may *not* be strange bedfellows. Once we realize, thanks to a logical behaviourist's close attention to the logic of our language about the mind, that we are not nearly as miraculous as many think, and once we appreciate, thanks to a philosophical naturalist's respect for science, that nature is much more wonderful than many think, Dennett figures that the reconciliation problem will dissolve quite easily.

The devil, of course, is in the details. The rest of this book provides detailed discussions of Dennett's attempts to reconcile specific features of the manifest image of persons with the scientific image of human nature. In the course of these projects,

Dennett proposes and defends dramatic and exciting new ways of addressing the oldest and deepest problems of philosophy. The following are among the questions he addresses. What is it for something to be real? What does it take for an organism to be conscious? Do animals have thoughts? What is the relation between thought and language? How is freedom possible in a world of causes? Dennett's treatments of these problems are provocative and insightful. Reader, prepare thyself: you are about to embark on a whirlwind tour of an exotic and exciting intellectual landscape!

Chapter Two

The intentional stance

Preamble

As we saw in chapter 1, a centrepiece of the manifest image of human beings is the practice of explaining human behaviour in terms of different kinds of thoughts, like beliefs and desires. Suppose Judy is avoiding Kate. A perfectly reasonable explanation is that she *believes* Kate intends to harm her, and she *desires* not to be harmed. But, as we have seen, if the sciences of human nature are on the right track, then anything a human being, like Judy, does, must be caused by states of her nervous system. So if the manifest and scientific images are to be reconciled, we must somehow explain how these two kinds of behavioural explanation are related. Judy does what she does because of what she believes and desires. She also does what she does because of the state of her nervous system. How are these two claims related?

There are several issues that arise when trying to answer this question. First, if both the scientific and the manifest images are correct, then there must be some distinction between physical systems, like clouds, that are not believers,[1] and physical systems, like human beings, that are believers. Any attempt to reconcile the manifest with the scientific images must explain what distinguishes physical systems that are believers from those that are not. A second problem that any attempt to reconcile the manifest with the scientific images must solve concerns determining *what* some believer believes. What scientific fact makes it the case that some believer believes that it is raining rather than believing that it is snowing?

Dennett proposes distinctive and controversial answers to these questions. In order to appreciate the details of Dennett's view and the controversy it has generated, it is useful to contrast it with a competing view: the proposal that beliefs are *identical* with sentences, formulated in a 'language of thought,' or 'mentalese,' that play specific causal roles in the brain (Fodor 1975). This is a form of what, in chapter 1, I called 'reductionism': it proposes to *identify* beliefs with brain states that have forms and functions analogous to lines of code in computer programming languages. The motivation behind this proposal is straightforward. Recall that beliefs are types of what philosophers call 'propositional attitudes'. This means that what a belief is about, its *content*, has a sentential form; it must be specified using a sentence. For example, the content of Judy's belief is specified using the sentence 'Kate intends to harm me'; the content of Judy's desire is specified using the sentence 'I am not harmed'. If the propositional attitudes are mentalese sentences in the brain, then the sentential form of their contents can be explained.

The mentalese theory of propositional attitudes implies straightforward answers to the two questions raised above. Proponents of the theory understand the distinction between physical systems that are believers and those that are not as one between systems that contain mentalese sentences playing appropriate roles and those that do not. Dennett proposes a different explanation of this distinction. With regard to the difference between having one belief, like the belief that it is raining, and another, like the belief that it is snowing, a mentalese reductionist might argue that a believer believes that it is raining when a mentalese translation of the sentence 'it is raining' plays the appropriate role in the believer. The believer believes that it is snowing when a mentalese translation of the sentence 'it is snowing' plays this role. Dennett's theory of belief includes a different solution to this problem.

My discussion in this chapter has four parts. First, I explain Dennett's theory of what beliefs are. Second, I explain how, on this understanding, the manifest practice of understanding intelligent behaviour in terms of beliefs relates to the scientific practice of understanding intelligent behaviour in terms of brain states. Third, I explore in greater detail the differences between Dennett's view and the mentalese view. Finally, I discuss some important criticisms of Dennett's view.

The three stances

The manifest concept of belief bears complicated connections to other concepts which are difficult to understand scientifically. Common sense tends to treat beliefs as inevitably or at least potentially conscious, so the manifest concept of belief is deeply connected to the manifest concept of consciousness. Some argue that, strictly speaking, you need to be a person to have full-blown beliefs, so the manifest concept of belief might be deeply connected to the manifest concept of person. Dennett tries to avoid such entanglements by focusing on a stripped-down concept of belief that captures important aspects of the common-sense concept, while ignoring some of these complicated connections to other concepts. In particular, he seeks to formulate a concept of belief that is independent of the concept of consciousness.

Recall from chapter 1 that the manifest concept of consciousness is particularly hard to reconcile with the scientific image: science is interested in objective, publicly accessible phenomena, but consciousness is supposed to be essentially subjective and private. According to Dennett, there is no way that the manifest concept of belief can be reconciled with the scientific image if it is not first extracted from its entanglements with the mysterious concept of consciousness. He tries to understand belief independently of consciousness, in objective, scientifically tractable terms, and then to explain consciousness in terms of this concept of belief.

To this end, Dennett proposes that believers are physical systems that can and sometimes must be explained using a certain predictive and explanatory strategy that he calls the 'intentional stance' (BS, p. 6; IS, p. 17). As I have explained, intentionality is a philosophical term for a property shared by all propositional attitudes; the property of standing for, or being about some object, situation or event. To adopt the intentional stance towards a physical system is to treat it as though it had states, like beliefs and other propositional attitudes, that are about objects, situations or events. The intentional stance is one of three predictive/explanatory strategies that one can use to explain certain complex, physical systems. The other two are the 'physical stance' (BS, pp. 4–5; IS, p. 16) and the 'design stance' (BS, p. 4; IS, pp. 16–17).

Dennett's three stances are best explained in the context of one of his favourite examples: the chess-playing computer (BS, pp. 4–7). According to Dennett, there are three basic ways of understanding a chess-playing computer. First, one can treat it as a purely physical system. That is, one can ignore the fact that it is designed to play chess, and simply treat it as a complicated physical object subject to the laws of physics. In principle, if you knew all the microscopic details about the internal state of a chess-playing computer, you could use the laws of physics to predict everything it would do in the future. If you looked at the electrical properties instantiated in all of its circuits and switches at one time, together with how they are related to each other, you could use our knowledge of electromagnetic phenomena to predict what happens next. Of course, we rarely do this. Trying to predict what one's computer will do next on the basis of its current physical state is practically impossible. However, sometimes we are forced to adopt this explanatory strategy. If the computer does not turn on, it may be because it is unplugged and, given the laws of physics, a computer without a power source cannot operate. Dennett calls this explanatory strategy the 'physical stance'. Whenever we explain and predict a system's behaviour on the basis of its physical states and the laws of physics, we are adopting the physical stance towards that system.

A second way of understanding some physical systems, especially artefacts and living things, is to assume that they are *designed* to fulfil some purpose, and then to predict that they will fulfil this purpose. For example, usually I do not need to know anything about the physical make-up of an alarm clock in order to know that it will ring at the time that I set. The clock is designed to do this and, usually, I need not bother understanding *how* it does this in order to predict or explain its behaviour. Chess-playing computers can be understood in this way as well. These are artefacts designed, by programmers, to fulfil some purpose. When there is no malfunction, one can predict and explain their behaviour by simply assuming that they will fulfil their purpose, without any knowledge of how they do this. This explanatory strategy can be applied to organisms and their organs as well. We can predict that a heart will pump blood without knowing anything about the physical details of how it does this. Dennett calls this explanatory strategy the 'design stance'. Whenever we explain or predict a system's behaviour based on the assumption that it will do what it is designed to do, we are adopting the design stance towards that system.

There are three important features of the design stance that I want to note. First, it is far more efficient than the physical stance. By this, I mean that it enables us to save enormous costs in time and energy when predicting complex systems. I do not need to waste any time and energy figuring out the internal configuration and state of an alarm clock in order to predict what it will do. I need only understand what the alarm clock is for, ignoring all of the physical details. Second, the design stance incorporates what philosophers might call a *normative* assumption. From the design stance, one predicts what a system will do based on what it *should* do. An alarm clock rings at the time you set because this is what it is *supposed* to do. Third, the design stance is *fallible*. It works as long as the system to which you apply it is functioning *properly* and certain enabling conditions are met. If the alarm clock is broken, or not plugged in or wound up, then the design stance will fail to predict what it will do: the clock will not ring at the time that you set. The second and third features are related: because the design stance relies on the normative assumption that systems do what they should do, if, for some reason, they cannot do what they should do, the design stance will fail to predict what they do. So, although the design stance enables tremendous savings in time and energy when predicting or explaining the behaviour of complex systems, it is an inherently *risky* stance: it depends on normative assumptions that sometimes fail to hold.

A third way of understanding some physical systems is to assume that they are *optimally* designed to fulfil some purpose, and then to predict that they will fulfil their purpose in an optimal way. Consider the chess-playing computer. In order to predict and understand its behaviour efficiently enough to play against it, even the design stance is too time-consuming. To predict a chess-playing computer's moves from the design stance, one would need to understand the details of the program the computer runs when playing chess. In other words, one would need to know the various functions the programmers intended the computer to execute, and predict that it will execute them. But chess-playing programs are incredibly complex, and often there is no way of uncovering their structure quickly. Rival software companies spend millions of dollars and thousands of person-hours trying to figure out each other's software. Fortunately, for those who play chess against computers, there is no need to do this. If one assumes that the computer is designed to play chess optimally, then one can ignore all the details of its programming, and simply predict that it will make the most optimal, or *rational* moves, given the goal of winning at chess. Dennett calls this explanatory strategy the 'intentional stance' because it involves attributing *intentional* states to a system. When one plays chess with a computer, one assumes that the computer *desires* to checkmate you and to avoid being checkmated. One also assumes that the computer *believes* that the different chess pieces are arranged in a particular configuration on the board, that there are certain rules for moving the pieces, and that certain moves increase its chances of winning or decrease its chances of losing.

The intentional stance, because it is a species of design stance, based on the assumption of optimal or rational design, exhibits the three features of the design stance I noted above. It enables enormous savings in efficiency, over both the physical and design stances, when predicting and explaining certain complex systems. In order to play chess with a computer, we need not know either the physical-level, 'hardware' properties of the computer, or the design-level 'software' properties of the chess-playing program it is running. By assuming that the computer wants to win, knows the rules of chess and the current board configuration, and distinguishes between good and bad moves, we can predict, with great success, how it will respond to our moves. The intentional stance makes an even more stringent normative assumption than the design stance: intentional systems are assumed to behave not only as designed, but in the most rational way possible. As a consequence, the intentional stance is even riskier than the design stance. The intentional stance yields false predictions not only when the system to which it applies fails to do what it is designed to do, but also when it fails to behave in the most rational way given its circumstances, due, for example, to sub-optimal design.[2] Nevertheless, when dealing with certain systems, especially human beings and sophisticated artefacts like computers, the risk is often worth it. Often, it is practically impossible to anticipate the behaviour of certain systems, quickly enough for it to make any difference, without assuming that they will choose the most rational course of action, given their goals and the information to which they have access.

Dennett notes that it is an objective fact that some systems are 'reliably and voluminously predictable via the intentional strategy' (IS, p. 15). In fact, it is impossible to understand some systems, including human beings, in any other way, simply because they are too difficult to explain and predict from the physical or the design stances. Dennett calls such systems 'intentional systems' (BS, p. 3). Whether or not something is an intentional system, according to Dennett, is a perfectly objective, third-person matter. Furthermore, Dennett's concept of an intentional system is not related to other scientifically problematic concepts in the way that the manifest concept of belief is (BS, p. 16). In order to determine whether a system counts as an intentional system, in Dennett's sense, we need not determine whether it is conscious nor what it is conscious of. We need not determine whether it is a person or not. All that matters is that, as a matter of fact, the best way of understanding it involves adopting the intentional stance towards it. Human beings, computers and at least some animals, on this view, count as intentional systems because there is no denying that the best and often only way of understanding their behaviour is by adopting the intentional stance: by assuming that they have goals and access to certain information, and that they decide on the most rational courses of actions given those goals and information.

After defining and explaining his technical notion of an intentional system, Dennett uses it to answer the philosophical questions regarding propositional attitudes raised above. According to Dennett, *all there is* to being a believer is being an intentional system. That is, any system that counts as an intentional system, in virtue of being reliably and voluminously predictable from the intentional stance, really is a believer (IS, p. 15). Furthermore, the specific beliefs and desires that the system contains are those that we must attribute to the system so that its behaviour turns out rational. To treat a system as an intentional system just is to treat it as perfectly rational. For this reason, the beliefs and desires we attribute to it are just those that *make sense* of its behaviour, that make its behaviour come out as the most rational course of action available (BS, pp. 5–9; IS, pp. 17–20).

Suppose, for example, we see a dog barking at a tree, after chasing a squirrel to the vicinity of the tree. If we treat the dog as an intentional system, we must attribute beliefs and desires to it that make the dog's barking at the tree the most rational course of action. Accordingly, even if the squirrel is actually up a different tree, we must attribute the following sorts of intentional states to it: the dog believes the squirrel is up the tree at which it is barking; the dog desires to catch the squirrel, and the dog believes that barking at the tree might help it catch the squirrel (either because it will scare the squirrel, or attract the attention of its master who will help catch the squirrel, or for some other reason). This set of propositional attitudes makes sense of the dog's behaviour; they make the dog's barking at the tree appear as a rational course of action. Suppose we attributed a different set of beliefs to the dog; suppose we assumed that the dog believed the squirrel was in a tree other than that at which the dog barked. This would not make sense of the dog's behaviour; it would not make the dog's barking at the tree appear rational. So, on Dennett's view, we know that this is *not* among the dog's beliefs. To treat the dog as an intentional system is to attribute beliefs and other intentional states to it that make its behaviour come out rational. According to Dennett, this is a sufficient constraint for determining precisely which intentional states it has.[3]

This feature of Dennett's view, that we must attribute beliefs and desires that make an intentional system's behaviour turn out rational, contains the seeds of a solution to one of the central aspects of the reconciliation problem. Recall from chapter 1 that many of the beliefs and desires we attribute to persons are about objects, situations and events that do not exist. Many children believe that Santa Claus brings gifts on Christmas Eve, for example. This feature of the manifest concept of belief is hard to reconcile with the scientific image because our behaviour is actually caused by brain states, and it is hard to see how real, concrete brain states could possibly be related to objects that do not exist. But if, as Dennett argues, beliefs attributed from the intentional stance must make sense of a person's behaviour, that is, make it turn out rational, then beliefs about things that do not exist do not seem so mysterious. Some physical systems, including human beings and animals, act in ways that can only be made sense of on the assumption that they believe in things that do not exist. The only belief attribution that makes sense of children's eager anticipation on Christmas Eve, that makes this and related behaviour turn out rational, is the belief that Santa is on his way. Dennett argues that the rationality assumption governing the intentional stance enables us to construct 'notional worlds,' that is, the subjective or mental worlds in which intentional systems live, populated by notional objects, that may or may nor correspond to real objects (IS, pp. 152–3). Many children live in notional worlds that contain the notional object, Santa Claus.

We now have, in outline, Dennett's solution to a central component of what, in chapter 1, I called the reconciliation problem. Dennett reconciles the manifest concept of belief with the scientific image in the following way. Some physical systems are very complex yet appear to be designed to fulfil certain purposes. Among these systems, there is a class whose behaviour can be reliably and voluminously predicted by assuming that they engage in the most rational behaviour given their goals and the information to which they have access. These are intentional systems. Any physical system that is an intentional system is a believer. Furthermore, the specific propositional attitudes that it has are determined in the following way: we assume that the system has goals and access to information that make its behaviour turn out rational. These goals count as the system's desires, and the items of information to which it has access count as its beliefs. It is important to emphasize that this appears to provide an analysis of the manifest concept of belief that is scientifically tractable: whether or not a system counts as an intentional system, in Dennett's sense, appears to be a perfectly objective matter, and this matter is independent of potentially intractable issues like whether or not the system is conscious, what it is conscious of, and whether or not the system is a person.

Applying the intentional stance

Given that Dennett's aim is to find a place for concepts of the manifest image in the world of science, the question arises: what role should the intentional stance play in the scientific explanation of human behaviour? There is no doubt that treating certain systems as intentional systems is incredibly useful. As Dennett might put it, just try building a mousetrap, or beating a chess-playing computer, without it! But how do intentional descriptions of some system, be it a human being, a non-human animal, or a computer, relate to design- or physical-level descriptions of it?

Although treating certain systems as intentional is often the best or only way to *begin* explaining them, according to Dennett, we should never stop our explanatory projects at this level. Any time a theorist describes a system in intentional terms, she '*takes out a loan* of intelligence' (BS, p. 12). What this means is that she assumes something that needs further explanation. Complex systems, like computers and brains, are often described in intentional terms, for example, as processing *signals*, obeying *commands*, or sending *messages*. Signals, commands, messages and other such phenomena are intentional events: they have *content*, that is, they stand for objects, events or situations. Though it often seems that such intentional descriptions leave nothing to explain, Dennett argues that they are seriously incomplete. According to Dennett, such descriptions presuppose signal-*readers*, *commanders* and message-*senders* (BS, p. 12). In other words, to use a term introduced in chapter 1, they presuppose homunculi. The goal of any science of human behaviour is to *explain* human capacities. Among these are the capacity for intelligence and other intentional phenomena, but if such capacities are 'explained' in terms of the capacities of intelligent homunculi, then nothing has been accomplished. This is why Dennett thinks that any intentional description of a system, no matter how apparently innocent and explanatory, takes out a loan of intelligence: such descriptions presuppose what the science of human behaviour is supposed to explain, namely, the human capacity for intelligent behaviour.

How does Dennett propose that scientists investigating intelligent behaviour repay the loans of intelligence they inevitably take when initially describing intelligent systems from the intentional stance? According to Dennett, there is nothing wrong with explaining some intelligent capacity of some system in terms of the capacities of component homunculi, *as long as the homunculi are all less intelligent than the system being explained.* That is, as long as the capacity being explained is explained as somehow emerging from the cooperative activity of multiple components with more limited capacities, then the loan of intelligence is being repaid (BS, pp. 122–4; SD, p. 137). For example, the capacity of the human visual system to construct a three-dimensional model of the world based solely on stimulations of the retina requires a kind of intelligence. As we saw in chapter 1, this capacity cannot be explained in terms of a homunculus somewhere in the brain that uses an *equally intelligent* visual system to process information projected, through the eyes, onto some analogue of a monitor. However, as some classic research paradigms in cognitive science assume,[4] this capacity may be explicable in terms of the cooperative activity of many more limited capacities,[5] requiring less intelligence.

In Dennett's terms, explanation in cognitive science, and other sciences of human nature, should proceed as a kind of 'cascade' (IS, p. 227) through the three stances that we can take towards complex systems. We start with a description from the intentional stance, wherein the system is treated as rational and optimally designed. The inevitable loans of intelligence made at this level are repaid when we explain how a physical system might be *designed* to approximate this rational ideal. In particular, we show how the cooperative activity of less rational, more limited components, designed to accomplish more limited goals, can in some circumstances yield system-level behaviour that appears rational. Here, we descend from an intentional stance description of the whole system to design stance descriptions of its components.

For example, an ideally rational chess-playing computer could always make the guaranteed best possible move, given the goal of checkmating its opponent or avoiding checkmate, and its knowledge of the current board position and the rules of chess. However, no physically possible chess player, human or computer, could always make the guaranteed best possible move, because the space of possible countermoves and counter-countermoves is too vast to explore in a realistic span of time. For each of the half-dozen or so moves permitted by the rules in one turn, one must consider the half-dozen or so possible responses on the part of the opponent, and then one's own responses to those responses, etc. Physically possible chess players do not have the time to consider all of these possibilities. Instead, they rely on *heuristics*, or rules of thumb, like 'Do not get the Queen out early', that enable them to approximate ideally rational chess playing. Such heuristics are implemented by component homunculi that are less intelligent than the overall system: rather than being designed to play chess, each is designed to detect some specific, limited set of situations, and execute a specific, limited set of responses to those situations. When we explain the apparently rational chess-playing competence highlighted in the intentional stance description of such a system, in terms of heuristics implemented by such limited component homunculi, we have descended to the design stance, in an attempt to repay our loans of intelligence.

This process can continue for each of these more limited homunculi, until we arrive at a level of description where the job performed by each homunculus can be performed by a thoroughly unintelligent physical system. For example, in the case of a digital computer, we arrive at a level of description where all that is going on is the flipping of switches between an 'on' position and an 'off' position, giving us the binary language of 1's and 0's. At this point, we have reached a physical stance description of the system. All loans of intelligence have been repaid, and the manifest concepts employed at the highest, intentional stance description have been reconciled with the scientific concepts of the physical stance (BS, pp. 122–4; SD, p. 137).

Dennett's view of how the intentional stance relates to other ways of describing systems in the explanation of intelligent behaviour is inspired by standard methodologies in computer science and cognitive science. When programmers develop software, they begin with a high-level, intentional stance description of the task they want the computer to perform. For example, they conceive of a chess-playing program as aiming to win chess games. They then descend to what some call the 'algorithmic level': they come up with instructions, executable by components of computers, that, together, can approximate chess playing competence. Finally, they develop ways of implementing these instructions in the physical hardware of actual computers. Cognitive science often employs a similar methodology. Natural cognitive systems, like human beings and non-human animals, are treated as computers running software that must be reverse-engineered. First, we determine, from what Dennett calls the intentional stance, the intelligent competence that we want to explain. Then, we hypothesize more limited capacities that cooperate to approximate the competence we want to explain. Finally, we investigate how these more limited capacities might be physically implemented in biological brains. This methodology has been self-consciously espoused by many researchers in cognitive science and artificial intelligence. Dennett is merely applying this common approach to explaining intelligence to the philosophical problem of reconciling the manifest with the scientific images.

The intentional stance vs. the language of thought hypothesis

In various places, Dennett speculates regarding the kinds of component homunculi that will be discernible in the human brain from the design stance. In other words, he speculates about how the human brain manages to approximate the rationality apparent in intentional stance descriptions of human beings. Dennett's philosophical views do not imply any answers to such questions; these are strictly empirical issues for Dennett, and a virtue of his proposal is that it is compatible with many different answers to such empirical questions. In fact, Dennett has changed his mind on this issue as new empirical facts have come to light. Early on, he joined Fodor in speculating that the brain might approximate intentional stance descriptions in virtue of running a language of thought, much like digital computers run programming languages (IS, p. 34). More recently, he has proposed that brains make use of cognitive processes that are often not language-like at all (BC, pp. 91–2). I bring these speculations up because they reveal an important strength of Dennett's philosophical proposals, and make clear his non-reductionist approach to reconciling the manifest with the scientific images.

The strength of Dennett's understanding of belief and other propositional attitudes in terms of the intentional stance is that it offers a welcome neutrality regarding empirical developments in the cognitive sciences. The intentional stance explains *what it is* to be a believer; it does not take a stand on *how* the human brain achieves this status. This sort of neutrality is welcome because, as a result, our status as believers is not dependent on empirical trends in science. Whatever science discovers about the brain, on Dennett's view we will remain intentional systems and, therefore, believers. This is because, no matter what, it will remain the case that human behaviour is reliably and voluminously predictable from the intentional stance. Given that Dennett's aim is to reconcile the manifest with the scientific images of human nature, this neutrality is important, since there is no telling what science will discover about the human brain. Other approaches to reconciliation, such as Fodor's reductionist proposal that propositional attitudes should be *identified* with mentalese sentences playing appropriate roles in the brain, forsake this kind of neutrality: such proposals must countenance the possibility that science will discover that we are not actually believers (IS, p. 93).[6] If such reductionism is the only kind of reconciliation available, this leaves components of the manifest image, like the propositional attitudes, open to arguments for elimination based on the latest empirical information about the brain (Churchland 1981).

It is also worth noting what motivates Dennett's anti-reductionism. Dennett's understanding of believers as intentional systems relies on the intuition that we would treat any system with certain capacities as a believer, no matter what went on inside them that explained these capacities. According to Dennett, we should not identify beliefs with mentalese sentences for the same reason that we should not identify beliefs with neurochemical states. Just as an organism made out of chemically different substances than human beings could still count as a believer in virtue of the way it behaved, on Dennett's view, human beings running different mentalese programs in their brains, or an organism *not running anything like* mentalese in its brain, could all count as believers, and as believing the same things (IS, pp. 66–7). Not only is this useful to the project of reconciling the manifest with the scientific images, it appears to agree with common sense: if one can interact with a system, be it another organism, an alien, or a computer, in the same way that one can interact with human beings one knows to have beliefs, what possible difference could their internal organization make? Would we not take them to be believers no matter what we found out about the way their brains were organized?

One way of understanding the difference between Dennett's view of belief and the view of a mentalese reductionist like Fodor is to distinguish two kinds of questions that are often conflated. There is a difference between asking, for example, what *makes* someone a husband, and asking how someone *comes to be* a husband. The first is a question of *definition*. What makes someone a husband is, partly at least, that he is recognized as such by the appropriate authorities. In most of the United States, a man counts as a husband just in case he is legally married to a woman. The second question is a question of *causation*: how did some particular person come to be a husband, that is, what caused him to marry a woman and thereby become a husband? This question has as many answers as there are husbands. Some are caused to be husbands by falling in love, others by their desire for resident status in a country, others by irate fathers with shotguns.

Similar questions can be asked about believers. We can ask: what makes something a believer? But we can also ask how something comes to be a believer. Dennett strongly distinguishes between these two questions (IS, pp. 43–4). According to Dennett, what makes a system a believer, in every case, is that the system is reliably and voluminously predictable from the intentional stance. However, what causes a system to achieve this status may vary from case to case. In one case it might be the fact that its brain runs mentalese much as a computer runs programming languages. In another case, it might be because its brain employs some other kind of cognitive process.

It is important to understand the distinction between questions of definition and questions of causation in order to make sense of Dennett's remarks about mentalese in some of his earlier writings. Dennett sometimes speculates that the only way a physical system *could* achieve the status of an intentional system is by running mentalese in the way that computers run programming languages (IS, p. 34). These remarks date from a time when the computer metaphor was the reigning paradigm in cognitive science. However, even at this time, Dennett was careful to distinguish his view from Fodor's. According to Fodor,[7] what it is to be a believer is to be controlled by a computer-like system that runs mentalese in the way that computers run programming languages. What it is to believe that snow is white is to have a mentalese translation of the English sentence 'snow is white' playing the appropriate role in one's brain. Dennett never bought into this view. Although he flirted with the view that the only mechanism capable of *causing* a system to behave as an intentional system, and therefore as a believer, is a computer-like brain running mentalese (IS, p. 34), Dennett never argued that this is what *made* a system a believer. On Dennett's view, what makes a system a believer is just its status as an intentional system. What causes a system to achieve this status is an open empirical question.

Criticisms of the intentional stance and responses

There are two major criticisms that have been raised against Dennett's proposal that to be a believer, in the fullest sense, is to be an intentional system, and to be an intentional system is to be reliably and voluminously predictable from the intentional stance. The first criticism questions Dennett's claim that to treat something as a believer one must treat it as ideally rational. The second criticism attempts to collapse Dennett's proposal into a kind of interpretationism (IS, p. 15), the view that belief is not an objective, scientific phenomenon, because what some subject believes is a matter of what some observer interprets the subject as believing. I conclude this chapter with a brief discussion of these criticisms and Dennett's responses to them.

The first criticism was forcefully articulated by Stephen Stich, in a published exchange with Dennett, not long after Dennett first proposed his thesis that believers are intentional systems (Stich 1982; IS, pp. 83–101). The problem, according to Stich, is that human beings often act irrationally, but they do not, except for in extreme circumstances, lose their status as believers when they act irrationally. Consider the case of the lemonade seller that forms the centrepiece of Stich and Dennett's debate. A child charges 12 cents for a cup of lemonade. You give her a quarter. She gives you 11 cents change. Her senses are functioning properly: she sees that you give her a quarter and that she gives you 11 cents; yet she still believes that she gives you the proper change. These sorts of mistakes happen all the time. They are examples of innocuous irrationality. There are also cases of extreme irrationality, for example, the insane. In such cases of irrationality, Stich agrees with Dennett: the concept of belief does not apply (Stich 1982, p. 50). Often, the insane are so irrational that there is no answer to the question of what they really believe. However, in everyday, innocuous cases of irrationality, such as giving the wrong change, Stich argues that this should not be our conclusion. Just because the child fails to give the correct change, we do not conclude that she lacks any of the relevant beliefs, or that she fails to be a believer.

Dennett is committed to the view that to treat someone as a believer is to treat them as an intentional system, and to treat someone as an intentional system is to treat them as ideally rational. Insofar as someone fails to be ideally rational, they fail to be an intentional system and, therefore, on Dennett's view, fail to be a true believer. It appears to follow that when the child produces the incorrect change, she is not, at the time, a true believer. How does Dennett respond?

Dennett thinks that the application of the intentional stance to a system is governed by at least three norms of rationality: (1) intentional systems have the beliefs they ought to have, that is, true and relevant beliefs, given their perceptual capacities and informational needs; (2) intentional systems have the desires they ought to have, given their biological needs; (3) intentional systems behave in ways that count as rational given these beliefs and desires (IS, p. 49). Dennett admits that true believers often have false beliefs, contrary to the first norm. However, on Dennett's view, in such cases, there is always a special story that explains the false belief, for example, a malfunctioning sense organ (IS, p. 18). The case of the lemonade seller is more complicated. By hypothesis, the lemonade seller's sense organs are functioning properly. She knows that (1) the lemonade costs 12 cents; (2) the customer gave her 25 cents; (3) she gave the customer 11 cents change; (4) $25-12 = 13$; (5) $25-12$ is equal to the correct change; (6) 11 is not equal to 13; yet she thinks that (7) she gave the customer the correct change (IS, pp. 85–6).

According to Dennett, this case shows that the intentional stance does not track what is really going on in a person's brain. It is an abstract 'standard' that we use to determine how best to interpret what is going on in someone's brain in intentional, manifest-image terms (IS, p. 92). Because any physical system, including a human being, only lives up to this standard imperfectly, lapses such as the lemonade sellers are inevitable. In such cases, it is impossible to say precisely what the person believes: there is good reason to maintain that the lemonade seller has all seven of the beliefs listed above, yet they appear to imply what Dennett calls 'brute irrationality too stark to countenance' (IS, p. 86). According to Dennett, the proper response is that the lemonade seller simply has an imperfect understanding of arithmetic and, therefore, given this lapse in rationality, the concepts of the intentional stance, including belief, apply only imperfectly: in this circumstance, the lemonade seller is not a true believer. We must abandon the intentional stance for a lower-level stance, like the design stance, to explain how the sub-optimal design of the child's brain leads to the irrational behaviour. This is precisely what we do when a chess-playing computer makes a stupid move: we conclude that the program's design must be sub-optimal.

However, this line of response has potentially perilous implications. Since no human being is ideally rational, does it not imply that human beings are not *really* intentional systems and, therefore, not *really* believers? And is this not to give up the attempt to reconcile the manifest with the scientific images, relegating the former to a second-class status? Dennett often insists that our rationality and, therefore, our status as intentional systems and true believers, are real because we are products of natural selection, and natural selection is bound to produce rational creatures, since rational creatures survive and reproduce better than irrational creatures (IS, p. 33). But, as Stich points out (1982, p. 52) and Dennett acknowledges (IS, p. 51), there is no guarantee that rational creatures will always survive and reproduce better than irrational creatures. For example, an animal that is paranoid, and does not wait until all the evidence is in to determine whether something moving in a bush is a predator, may have an advantage over an animal that carefully weighs all the evidence. On the other hand, it may be more rational, from the point of view of an animal's genes, to be paranoid, rather than wasting valuable resources on coming to the rationally most defensible decisions about the presence of predators (IS, pp. 96–7). As Dennett points out, rationality is a slippery notion. By the strict standards of logic and decision theory, humans are not generally rational.[8] However, Dennett is content to understand rationality as 'a general-purpose term of cognitive approval' (IS, p. 97). He argues that applying this standard to certain complex systems enables us to track 'real patterns' (BC, pp. 95–120) in their behaviour, especially when such systems are products of processes of selection, like evolution by natural selection. I return to these points in chapter 6, where I discuss Dennett's understanding of evolution and real patterns.

The second criticism commonly levelled at Dennett's proposal is that it collapses into a kind of interpretationism. Interpretationism, in this context, is the view that there are no true believers. The practice of attributing beliefs and desires to human beings, non-human animals, computers and other systems is like literary criticism: it is useful in some contexts; however, it is inevitably subjective and corresponds to nothing objectively true of such systems.

On Dennett's view, to be a believer is to be an intentional system, and to be an intentional system is to be reliably and voluminously predictable from the intentional stance. However, as Dennett acknowledges, almost any object in the world meets this condition. For example, while giving a talk on this topic at Oxford, Dennett asked his audience to consider the lectern at which he was speaking. Could we not attribute the following belief and desire to it, thereby making sense of its behaviour? The lectern desires to be at the centre of the English-speaking academic world, and believes that this is exactly where it is; therefore, it chooses to remain where it is. Our prediction is borne out: the lectern does not move. Does this mean the lectern is an intentional system? After all, it is reliably and voluminously predictable from the intentional stance. Dennett's response is that we have other ways of explaining why the lectern does not move. It is only for *some* systems, like human beings, non-human animals and computers, that the intentional stance is *indispensable*: we have no other way of predicting and explaining their behaviour (IS, p. 23). So, intentional systems are those systems that are reliably and voluminously predictable from the intentional stance, and that cannot be predicted or explained in any other way. But this move leaves Dennett open to the charge of interpretationism.

Here is why.[9] Suppose the earth is visited by an advanced race of Martians whose scientific powers are orders of magnitude greater than ours. To them, we appear as simple physical systems, comparable to the way thermostats appear to us. These Martians can predict everything we do, entirely from the physical stance. They have no need to take advantage of the efficiency of the design stance or the intentional stance in order to predict and explain what we do; their brains are so advanced that they can predict and explain everything we do, in the same way that we can predict and explain everything thermostats do. Although *to us* the intentional stance is an indispensable tool for the prediction and explanation of human behaviour, *to the Martians*, it is entirely dispensable. Given Dennett's response to the 'lectern problem', this appears to imply that, to the Martians, human beings are *not* intentional systems, while to other human beings they are. But is this not just a version of interpretationism? Whether or not something is an intentional system is not an objective matter at all, it seems. It is just a way of interpreting certain complex systems if one's brain is too limited to understand them physically; but if something's status as an intentional system depends, in this way, on the powers of whoever is trying to explain and predict it, then it is an entirely subjective matter. For some purposes (our own), we must be treated as intentional systems, but for other purposes (those of the Martians), we can be treated purely as physical systems. How is this different from interpreting poetry, which can be interpreted in one way for some purposes and in another way for other purposes?

This is a version of the most influential objection to Dennett's proposals concerning the manifest concepts of belief and other propositional attitudes. He is often accused of *instrumentalism*, the view that such concepts correspond to nothing objectively real, and are merely useful tools for predicting behaviour. Dennett wants to defend a view that is perched perilously on the fence between such instrumentalism and the 'industrial strength realism' (BC, p. 45) of the mentalese hypothesis, according to which beliefs are real, concrete, sentence-like brain states, as objective as bacterial infections:

> [B]elief is a perfectly objective phenomenon (that apparently makes me a realist), [however] it can be discerned only from the point of view of one who adopts a certain *predictive strategy*, and its

existence can be confirmed only by an assessment of the success of
that strategy (that apparently makes me an interpretationist).

(IS, p. 15)

To this end, he proposes a complicated and subtle reply to the
charge of instrumentalism. He claims that any explanation that
ignores our status as intentional systems and, therefore, as believers, misses *real patterns* in human behaviour.[10]

Even the Martians, with all of their scientific prowess, would
miss these real patterns if they treated us only as physical systems.
For example, consider the pattern we track when we attribute
beliefs and desires to traders at the New York Stock Exchange (IS,
p. 26). We can predict what they will do by hypothesizing what
they believe and desire. The Martians could predict the very same
behaviour on the basis of physical stance descriptions: looking
just at the brain states of some trader, and the physical states of her
environment, they could predict exactly the key strokes she would
punch on her computer to order some stock. However, the Martians would miss the fact that exactly the same transaction could
be accomplished in countless physically distinct ways. The trader
could use a phone to call in the trade, or use hand gestures to signal
the trade, etc. The fact that all of these count as the same action,
that is, making the same trade, would be lost on the Martians: it is
an abstract though real pattern that can be discerned only from
the intentional stance, and is therefore invisible from the physical
stance. So there would be something real missed even by Martian
super-scientists, if they did not apply the intentional stance to
human beings: if they did not treat us as believers. It is in this sense
that, according to Dennett, the manifest concepts of belief and
other propositional attitudes, as he understands them in terms of
the intentional stance, correspond to something objectively real in
the scientific image of the world.[11]

The way forward

From the earliest published versions of his proposals, Dennett has
defended a very specific strategy for solving the reconciliation

problem. The central concepts of the manifest image constitute an imposing, mutually reinforcing whole that appears to resist reconciliation with the scientific image: human beings are persons, who come to free, rational decisions, based on conscious beliefs and desires. Dennett's strategy for reconciling these concepts with the scientific image has, from the start, been to 'divide and conquer'. According to Dennett, the chink in the armour of the manifest image is intentionality: intentional states, like beliefs and desires, are easiest to reconcile with the scientific image. In this chapter, we have seen Dennett's proposed solution to this part of the reconciliation problem. But it is just a first step. Dennett's goal has always been to answer the following question: '[A]re there mental treasures that cannot be purchased with intentional coin?' (BS, p. 16). By this he means: can the other central concepts of the manifest image, consciousness, freedom of the will and personhood, be entirely understood in terms of intentional states like belief? If they can, then a solution to the reconciliation problem is possible: belief and other intentional states are understood in terms of the scientifically tractable concept of an intentional system, and other mental treasures are understood in terms of intentional states of various sorts.

In the next three chapters, I explain how Dennett attempts to 'pay' for the other mental treasures of the manifest image with the currency of the intentional stance. Chapters 3 and 4 explain Dennett's theory of consciousness and the self. Chapter 5 explains his theory of personhood and freedom of the will.

According to Dennett, his view of the intentionality of mental states, like beliefs, differs from the received philosophical view in a single, fundamental respect. As we saw in chapter 1, most philosophers make a distinction between *derived* and *intrinsic* intentionality. The apparent intentionality of artefacts, for example, the fact that the word 'cat' stands for cats, is derived from the intentions of human designers and users. However, on the received view, the intentionality of these very intentions, and other human mental states, can derive from nothing: human mental states must have intrinsic or *original* intentionality. Dennett thinks that original intentionality is a fundamentally mysterious and unscientific notion (IS, Ch. 8). According to Dennett, all intentionality, including the intentionality of human mental states, is derived. From where do human beings and other biological systems derive their intentionality? Dennett's answer is 'Mother Nature' (IS, p. 298), or, more specifically, evolution by natural selection. Systems that are products of a process of selection exhibit real patterns of behaviour that can only be tracked from the intentional stance. So their intentionality is derived from evolution by natural selection. And the process of natural selection itself can only be understood by taking the intentional stance towards Mother Nature. This means that chapter 2 has left out an important piece of the puzzle: Dennett's proposal for reconciling the manifest concepts of belief and intentionality with the scientific image depends to a large degree on his understanding of evolution. Chapter 6 is devoted to filling this lacuna.

Chapter Three

Escaping the Cartesian Theatre

Preamble

In chapter 1, I briefly discussed the different components of the manifest concept of consciousness that appear particularly hard to reconcile with the scientific image. One of them is the subjectivity on which Thomas Nagel (1974) focuses. Information about what it is like to be some person or organism is only available from the *subject's* perspective: the *first-person* perspective of that person or organism. This implies a second puzzling feature: where there is consciousness there must be a *self* that is conscious, a self that has access to information about what it is like. A third puzzling feature is what philosophers call the 'ineffability' of conscious experience. Information is ineffable if it cannot be conveyed in words. We can often express exactly what we *believe* in words: if I believe that *Napoleon Dynamite* is a great movie, then I can express this belief using these words. However, it seems impossible to express, as precisely, what it is like to *experience* something to someone who has not experienced it. For example, how does one express what it is like to visually experience bright red to a blind person? A fourth puzzling feature of consciousness concerns the apparent incorrigibility of persons regarding what it is like to be them. On the manifest understanding of consciousness, persons cannot be wrong about what they are consciously experiencing.

These four features are central to what Dennett calls the 'Cartesian Theatre' model of consciousness. According to this model, there is a place in the mind–brain where information first processed quickly and unconsciously gets re-presented for consciousness. This 'place' is like a theatre, or television monitor, where the data of consciousness are presented for the self to peruse. Only the self has access to this information (outside observers cannot see it), and the self cannot be wrong about what is presented in the Cartesian Theatre. Finally, this information cannot be expressed in words; it can only be fully appreciated first hand.

The Cartesian Theatre model of consciousness clearly rules out the possibility of studying consciousness scientifically. Not only is consciousness essentially subjective, in Nagel's sense; it also presupposes a homunculus! According to Dennett, there is no place in the brain where all the information comes together for the self to examine. Furthermore, there is no 'self' *in the brain*.[1] And even if there were, we could not *explain* a person's consciousness in terms of the fact that her 'self' is conscious of information in the Cartesian Theatre, because this would launch the kind of 'infinite regress' of homunculi that I discussed in chapter 1. The consciousness of the 'self' would have to be explained in terms of the consciousness of the 'self's self', and so on. If we are to take the scientific image at all seriously then, Dennett argues, the Cartesian Theatre model of consciousness must be abandoned.

Dennett proposes an alternative to the Cartesian Theatre model of consciousness, a scientifically tractable model he initially called the 'Multiple Drafts Model' (CE, p. 17), but more recently has called the 'fame in the brain' model (SD, p. 136). He also proposes a third-person, scientific methodology for studying human consciousness that he calls 'heterophenomenology' (CE, p. 72). This method is basically an application of the intentional stance to a subject's utterances about their own conscious states.

In this chapter, I first discuss some of the reasons philosophers are tempted by the Cartesian Theatre model of consciousness. I then explain Dennett's alternative model: first, I discuss his

third-person method for studying consciousness, heterophenomenology; second, I give a brief sketch of his alternative fame in the
brain model, in the course of which I explain some of his key reasons for abandoning the Cartesian Theatre model, and review his
response to one key reason that philosophers have offered in
favour of the Cartesian Theatre model. In chapter Four, I look at
Dennett's alternative in more detail. I also discuss his responses to
other reasons that have been offered against it and in favour of the
Cartesian Theatre model.

The Cartesian Theatre

Why is it so tempting to suppose that there is a place, in the brain,
where information that is initially processed unconsciously is
re-presented in a format that makes it inscrutable to outside
observers (i.e., subjective), impossible to fully express (i.e., ineffable), and allows the self incorrigible access? We discussed some
reasons in chapter 1. The way things appear is very different from
the way they are. Water can appear to change temperature, even if
it actually does not. Buildings can appear to shrink, even if they
actually do not. It is therefore tempting to posit a place where all of
these appearances exist, i.e., consciousness, or what some call
'phenomenal space'. This inference, though tempting, relies on
subtle and often undefended assumptions. It assumes that, since
the way things appear is different from the way they are, in addition to things in real space and time, there must also be *appearances* in *phenomenal* space and time. Furthermore, most thinkers
tempted by this inference assume that persons have a far more
intimate acquaintance with the appearances in phenomenal space
and time than with the things in real space and time. The reason
for this is the common-sense practice of treating people as incorrigible about the way things appear to them: you can be wrong
about whether *there actually was* a knock at the door, but you
cannot, typically, be wrong about *whether there appeared to you to
be* a knock at the door. So, goes this line of thinking, you must have
intimate, incorrigible knowledge of the phenomenal space and
time in which the appearance of the knock took place.

Dennett is part of an influential tradition in twentieth century philosophy that explicitly resists this line of argument.[2] However, unlike earlier representatives of this tradition, he focuses on *facts we know about the nervous system* in order to criticize it and to offer an alternative. Given that the supposed phenomenal space and time of appearances is distinct from real space and time, and that persons have intimate access to it, it stands to reason that phenomenal space and time, filled with appearances, exist *within* the minds of persons. But, if we assume that science is correct that all human behaviour is caused by the nervous system, then the mind must somehow arise from the activity of the nervous system. So, phenomenal space and time, together with the appearances it contains, must somehow exist within the activity of the nervous system, but as we saw in chapter 1, and as Dennett argues repeatedly and at length, there is no property of the nervous system fit for the job of 'housing' phenomenal space and time. Nevertheless, philosophers have proposed further reasons in support of the claim that phenomenal space and time, i.e., the Cartesian Theatre, must exist.[3]

Philosophers who defend the Cartesian Theatre and, more broadly, the reality of the world of appearances, tend to appeal to certain very strong *intuitions*.[4] As we have seen, Nagel (1974) appeals to the intuition that no amount of information about a bat's nervous system can reveal what it is like to be a bat. Another common intuition (Chalmers 1996, p. 94) appeals to the following possibility. Imagine an entity that is identical to you in every scientifically detectable way. This entity has all the same physical properties as you: the same mass, the same height, the same number and organization of cells, the same brain, the same states of activation in its neurons, etc. Because of this, this entity's behaviour is indistinguishable from your behaviour. When you cough, this entity coughs; when you sigh, this entity sighs, etc. According to the intuitions of many philosophers, despite all of these similarities, it is possible that this entity, unlike you, is *not conscious*. The philosophical term of art for such a physical duplicate is 'zombie'. Zombies are physical duplicates of conscious persons, which are, nevertheless, not conscious. It is important to keep in mind the distinction between philosophers' zombies and the kinds of zombies depicted in movies. Zombies in movies are not philosophers' zombies because they are not physical duplicates of conscious persons: their *physical* behaviour, e.g., the way they walk, is obviously different from that of normal conscious persons. But philosophical zombies are supposed to be perfect physical duplicates of conscious persons, which are not conscious.[5]

Philosophers have coined a term of art for the properties that we have and that our zombie duplicates lack: 'qualia'. These are supposed to be the *intrinsic* properties of experience. An intrinsic property is a property that an object or state has independently of its relations to any other objects or states, e.g., independently of its causes, effects or dispositions (SD, pp. 78–9, 177). The experiences of our zombie duplicates have all the same causes, effects and dispositions as our experiences: that is why they behave exactly as we do. When the pattern of light reflected off an apple hits your and your zombie twin's retinas, your brains go into exactly the same states, precipitating exactly the same brain activity and causing exactly the same responses, e.g., reaching for and taking a bite out of the apple. So the difference between us and our zombie duplicates, what we have and they lack, must be the intrinsic properties of experience, i.e., qualia. And since this difference consists in the fact that we are conscious of appearances and our zombie duplicates are not, some philosophers conclude that appearances presented in consciousness, i.e., the way red looks, the way roses smell, the way chocolate tastes, etc., are qualia, that is, intrinsic properties of experience.

So, we can reconstruct the following philosophical argument in support of the Cartesian Theatre, based on the intuition that philosophical zombies are really possible. A person is identical to her zombie twin in all physical, including all neural, respects, but while a person is conscious, her zombie twin is not. So, a person's consciousness cannot consist in any physical or neural properties. Rather, it must consist in certain intrinsic, non-physical properties of her experiences, or qualia. Therefore, any facts about the brain that appear at odds with what we intuitively take qualia or appearances to be are irrelevant. It follows that, for all science says, qualia or appearances exist and are exactly as we take them to be.

Since qualia or appearances appear on the stage of the Cartesian Theatre for the self to peruse, science can provide no evidence that this is not the case.

Here is another influential line of thought in defence of the Cartesian Theatre. According to some philosophers, we need not rely on the bare intuition that zombies are possible to argue that science has nothing to say about the world of appearances. Instead, we may rely on the following thought experiment (Jackson 1982). Consider Mary, a neuroscientist of the future. Mary is the 'Einstein' of cognitive neuroscience: she knows *everything* there is to know about the human nervous system and how it works. She is so good, that, given any stimulus to any sense organ – light reflected off a work by Van Gogh, an aroma emanating from a vintage Merlot, the sound of Vladimir Horowitz playing Chopin, the text of *War and Peace*, etc. – she can predict exactly which state the brain of any person will enter when exposed to that stimulus. Furthermore, she can predict the exact effects that this state will have on the person's brain and behaviour in the future. So, for example, given a scan of Lucy's current brain state, she can predict that Lucy will eventually wince and utter 'How grotesque!' when her retina is stimulated by light reflected off one of Van Gogh's self-portraits. The catch is that Mary has acquired all of her hard-won knowledge of the brain in an environment devoid of colour, perhaps because she has been locked in a room filled entirely with black and white objects,[6] or because her colour vision system has been reversibly disabled. This possibility raises the following question: does Mary know what it is like to see red (or any other colour)? Or, equivalently, suppose we release Mary from her black and white environment and she experiences colour for the first time; will she *learn something new*? Will she be *surprised*?

If, like most people, you think that Mary will learn something new, then what science tells us about the nervous system is irrelevant to evaluating the Cartesian Theatre as a model of consciousness. This is because, by hypothesis, prior to being released from her black and white environment, Mary knows *everything* that science could possibly discover about the nervous system. However, upon her release, she *learns something new*, namely, what it is like to see colours. So what it is like to see colours is something over and above what science can discover about the nervous system. The world of appearances, or, as philosophers call them, qualia, is beyond the ken of science. If, intuitively, qualia appear on the stage of the Cartesian Theatre, for the self to peruse, there is nothing that science can discover about the nervous system that could throw this model into jeopardy.

Dennett responds to these arguments in the course of developing his own alternative methodology for the scientific study of consciousness, as well as his own model of consciousness. In the following, I focus on explaining Dennett's alternative methodology and model. I review some of Dennett's responses to arguments in favour of the Cartesian Theatre at the end of this chapter and in chapter 4.

Heterophenomenology

As we have seen, one of the primary obstacles to a science of consciousness is its alleged privacy or subjectivity. The data of consciousness, qualia, or the way things appear, are supposed to be invisible to all but the conscious subject. How is a science even supposed to start if it has no way of representing the data it needs to explain in objective, third-person terms (SD, p. 148)?

Many philosophers have supposed that the only way to access the data of consciousness is through introspection by a subject of her own conscious states.[7] Some (Husserl 1982) claim that it is possible to develop a rigorous, introspection-based methodology for studying consciousness. Husserl's term for this is 'phenomenology,' or the study of *phenomena*, which, to him, meant the study of the world of appearances. Husserl's goal was to bracket or ignore what he knew of the real world with the aim of discovering truths about the world of appearances, considered by themselves.

Dennett argues that phenomenology is not a good method for studying consciousness (CE, pp. 66–8). The primary reason is that there are no public constraints on a person's judgements about what they introspect. It is well known that persons tend to exhibit what psychologists call 'confirmation bias' (Wason 1960). We tend to seek out or notice evidence that confirms our theories and expectations, and ignore evidence that disconfirms them. Science counteracts this tendency by demanding that evidence be inter-subjectively verifiable. If you claim there is evidence for some theory of yours, it must be possible for me, and others, to verify this claim by looking at the same evidence, e.g., by replicating some experiment. But since no one but you can access your world of appearances, your qualia, there is no way of verifying what you say about them. So, phenomenology is inadequate as a scientific methodology: subjects tend to introspect exactly what their theories lead them to expect.[8]

This problem with phenomenology leads to a dilemma: either we ignore one of the central features of consciousness, namely, the subject's special access to the way things appear to them, or we abandon the dream of a science of consciousness. One of Dennett's foremost contributions is his proposal of a method for studying consciousness that, according to him, evades this dilemma. He calls this method 'heterophenomenology'. The prefix 'hetero' means 'other'. Dennett proposes a method of doing phenomenology for another, or, put another way, a method for studying any subject's world of appearances from the outside. The goal is to find a way of describing a subject's world of appearances from the third person. This would constitute a publicly accessible specification of the data of consciousness, against which any theory of consciousness could be evaluated. If heterophenomenology works, then our theories of consciousness can be constrained by public verification, and a sci-ence of consciousness should be possible.

How is heterophenomenology supposed to work? We simply give a conscious subject the benefit of the doubt when they talk about how things appear to them. As we have seen in the previous two chapters, utterances of natural language are examples of *intentional* events: they stand for or represent things as being a certain way. Given Dennett's understanding of intentionality in terms of the intentional stance, he has a clear method for inter-preting noise coming out of a subject's mouth as an utterance of natural language and, therefore, an intentional event: we must treat the utterance as expressing a belief that fits into a system of other intentional states, which makes sense of the subject's overall behaviour, i.e., which makes the subject's overall behaviour come out *rational*. Consider a child who utters the sentence 'Santa is coming tonight.' As we saw in chapter 2, the only way to make sense of such verbal behaviour, and related non-verbal behaviour, is by assuming that the child is expressing the belief that Santa is coming tonight. It does not matter that this belief is false because Santa does not exist. Sometimes we have to attribute beliefs in things that do not exist to a subject in order to make her behaviour come out rational. Recall from chapter 2 that this method of interpretation leads to the construction of a subject's *notional world*, the subjective world in which the subject lives, populated by all sorts of *notional objects*, that may or may not correspond to real objects. Heterophenomenology is an application of this method of interpretation to a subject's utterances about their own conscious states, about their world of appearances.

According to Dennett, when we ask a subject about how things appear to them, their responses enable us to generate the subject's 'heterophenomenological world' (CE, p. 81). A subject's heterophenomenological world is a *part* of their notional world: while the latter consists of *all* objects the subject takes to exist and *all* facts they take to be true, the former consists of all objects they take to exist *in their conscious mind* and all facts they take to be true *of their conscious mind*. There is a distinction between constructing a subject's heterophenomenological world and constructing the rest of their notional world. In the latter case, our interpretation of the subject's thoughts and utterances is constrained *only* by the rationality assumption: we ascribe those beliefs that make their overall behaviour come out as rational, *whether or not the subject is aware of these beliefs*. For example, even if the subject denies that they believe that their mother wishes to harm them, if ascribing this belief enables us to make sense of most of their behaviour, e.g., involuntary shudders when their mother walks by, then we must assume that in the subject's *notional* world, their mother wishes to harm them. However, in constructing the subject's heterophenomenological world, our interpretation must answer to a further constraint: since our aim is to do justice to the subject's

allegedly incorrigible access to their conscious experience, interpretation is also constrained by the assumption that the subject is
authoritative about how things appear to them.[9] Accordingly, in
the above example, in the subject's *heterophenomenological* world,
their mother does *not* wish to harm them. This is because, recall,
the subject denies that their mother wishes to harm them.

Constructing a subject's heterophenomenological world,
according to Dennett, is rather like constructing the fictional
world of a novel. In the latter case, we treat the *author's* words as
authoritative: if J. R. R. Tolkien writes that hobbits have hairy feet,
then this is automatically true of 'Middle Earth', the fictional world
of the *Hobbit* and the *Lord of the Rings*. Similarly, in the former
case, we treat the *subject's* utterances as authoritative: if the subject
says that their vision is just as acute at the centre of their visual field
as at the peripheries, then this is automatically true of the subject's
heterophenomenological world (SD, p. 41).

Heterophenomenology is neutral about whether such facts are
also true of the *real* world of the subject's nervous system. This is
something for science to discover. At this point, we are only interested in specifying the *data* to be explained by a science of consciousness in a third-person way. And, according to Dennett, the
way to do this is to treat the subject's utterances as authoritative,
and interpret them *as if* they express truths about the subject's
mind. This enables us to generate the subject's heterophenomenological world.

The first important feature to note about the method of heterophenomenology is that it is entirely third-person, or objective.
It is anchored in what a subject utters, and this is something that is
intersubjectively verifiable. We simply need to make a *transcript* of
the subject's utterances, and this text serves as the authoritative
source on the basis of which their heterophenomenological world
is constructed, much like Tolkien's novels serve as the authoritative source on the basis of which Middle Earth is constructed. Of
course, there is room for error and disagreement, both in interpreting a subject's utterances about her own conscious states and
in interpreting fiction. However, this does not disqualify either as
a third-person, objective endeavour: there is room for error and

disagreement in interpreting the results of experiments and measurements in the physical sciences as well. Journalists and court stenographers routinely interpret utterances of subjects, and arrive at impressive consensus about what subjects say. Transcripts of what subjects say can therefore act as constraints on interpretation. Contextual factors, like where the subject is when they make an utterance, who they are talking to, their intentions, history, etc., are all relevant to arriving at the best possible interpretation of a subject's utterances from the intentional stance. This is a difficult process with plenty of potential pitfalls that need to be avoided. However, it is entirely intersubjective: the kinds of considerations that favour one interpretation of some transcript over another can be appreciated by diverse researchers, who can appeal to them in reasoned debate and, eventually, arrive at consensus interpretations.

The second important feature to note about the method of heterophenomenology is that it is metaphysically minimalist and neutral (CE, p. 95). It is metaphysically minimalist in the same way that the intentional stance is metaphysically minimalist: it does not make any strong assumptions about what *really* exists. Heterophenomenology simply assumes that a subject's utterances can be interpreted *as if* they are about a world of appearances that have certain properties. It makes no assumptions about whether this world of appearances is real or not. The heterophenomenological worlds generated in this way are *merely hypothetical*. The metaphysical *neutrality* of heterophenomenology consists in this. It takes no stand on the real, metaphysical status of the entities and facts of which subjects speak.

Dennett draws a very useful analogy to anthropology in order to dramatize this point (CE, pp. 82–5). When investigating the mythology of some tribe, an anthropologist must construct a canonical account of the mythical world the tribe takes to exist. In order to do this, they must treat the natives' utterances about this mythical world as authoritative: the mythical world is as they say it is. But, the anthropologist need not *endorse* the natives' point of view. Whether there is good reason to think that the mythical world corresponds to reality is a separate question. But before this question is addressed, the anthropologist must construct a clear account of what the mythical world is supposed to be. In doing this, they must treat the natives as authoritative and, at the same time, remain neutral about the truth of what they say. Heterophenomenology is the application of this anthropological method to any subject's utterances about their own conscious mind.

Heterophenomenology is neutral in a more specific way as well. Above, we saw that a major philosophical reason for accepting the Cartesian Theatre model of the conscious mind is the alleged possibility of philosophical zombies. Supposedly, consciousness is independent of what science discovers about the nervous system because it is possible for an entity to be physically identical to a conscious person without being conscious. Heterophenomenology is neutral on the question of whether this is really possible and on the question of whether a specific subject is a zombie or not. This is because, from the perspective of heterophenomenology, there is no difference between conscious persons and their zombie duplicates. A heterophenomenological world is generated on the basis of one's verbal behaviour. Since verbal behaviour is *physical*, any verbal behaviour engaged in by a conscious person is also engaged in by their zombie duplicate. As a result, conscious persons generate exactly the same transcripts, and hence, exactly the same heterophenomenological worlds as their zombie duplicates. For this reason, heterophenomenology is neutral on whether a given subject is a zombie or not, and on whether zombies are even really possible or not (CE, p. 95).

It should be clear from the foregoing how Dennett avoids the dilemma facing the science of consciousness, discussed above. How can the intersubjective methodology of science do justice to the first-person authority that we take subjects to have regarding their conscious experiences? By applying heterophenomenology. This method *assumes* that subjects are authoritative about their conscious experiences. So it does justice to the first-person access common sense takes subjects to have to their conscious experience. Anything that subjects say about their conscious experience must be true *of their heterophenomenological worlds*. This includes some of the problematic properties of the manifest concept of consciousness, noted above. If a subject says their conscious experiences are *ineffable*, then this is taken to be true of her heterophenomenological world and, consequently, it is a datum that any science of consciousness must explain, *in one way or another*. The same goes for the claim that consciousness requires a unified self that observes appearances as though on a stage. Heterophenomenology does justice to the fact that many subjects *believe* their experience to be this way. And it acknowledges an obligation to explain why subjects *believe* this. However, its metaphysical neutrality allows scientists to explore different theories for explaining such beliefs: though the subject is treated as authoritative regarding what they *believe* about their conscious mind, they are *not* treated as authoritative about what their conscious mind is *really* like; such judgements require intersubjective verification by the methods of science.

For this reason, heterophenomenology avoids the problems with traditional phenomenology: it incorporates intersubjective constraints both on the specification of the data of consciousness, and on the construction of theories of them. A subject's heterophenomenological world must be anchored in the interpretation of public transcripts of her utterances. Furthermore, theorists must remain neutral on whether the denizens of a subject's heterophenomenological world correspond to anything real in the subject's nervous system. The subject's theories about what is going on inside their conscious mind have no privileged status. Just as members of some tribe may be wrong about the rain god, a subject may be wrong about their world of appearances. It is up to intersubjectively constrained science to come up with the best theoretical explanation of the data generated by heterophenomenology.

Fame in the brain

According to Dennett, many of the central features of subjects' heterophenomenological worlds are illusions. When we construct a heterophenomenological world based on transcripts of the typical subject's utterances about how things appear to them, this world looks pretty much like the Cartesian Theatre.[10] There appears to be a single unified self making all the decisions based on appearances about which it cannot be mistaken, to which no one else has access, and which cannot be expressed in words. However, just because this is what many subjects *believe* about how their minds work, does not make it true. Just as members of some Amazon tribe may earnestly believe in a rain god, many subjects earnestly believe that their minds are Cartesian Theatres. In both cases there are good reasons to doubt these beliefs. Science rules out the possibility of supernatural entities like rain gods, and neuroscience rules out the possibility that the mind is a Cartesian Theatre.

As we have seen, if the mind is what controls behaviour, then the mind is some pattern of organization in the nervous system, but the nervous system contains no central system with incorrigible access to ineffable appearances, on the basis of which it makes decisions about what to do next. Rather, the nervous system is better seen as a complex collection of numerous computational agents operating at the same time, or *in parallel*. None of these agents knows what the whole system is doing, and each has only limited access to what the others are doing. The nervous system is rather like a *social entity* – a city for example. How does New York feed its citizens every day? There is no central authority that plans all the details. A solution to this task emerges from myriad local interactions, taking place in parallel, among millions of producers, suppliers, retailers and customers, none of which has any access to what most of the others are doing.

If this is what subjects' minds are actually like, then why does heterophenomenology yield the illusion of the Cartesian Theatre? Why do people think that their minds consist of unified selves that make decisions based on ineffable appearances to which these selves have incorrigible access? How does such an illusion arise from the tumult of parallel processing that actually constitutes the mind? Dennett's theory must answer these questions: it must *explain* the heterophenomenological data, even though it assumes that much of it is illusory. This is the central burden of Dennett's theory, and I explore his answers to these questions in detail in chapter 4. Here, I provide a mere sketch of what is to come.

According to Dennett, the illusion of a central executive in charge of the mind–brain emerges, roughly, in the following way.

As you go about your daily business, your brain is a hotbed of activity of which you are mostly oblivious. Consider the well-known phenomenon of driving 'on automatic pilot'. If you take the same road to work every day, you will not notice most of the information your brain processes in order to control your driving: you will not notice that some door of a building you pass has been repainted, that there is a new pothole just past the intersection, etc. However, if your brain is appropriately *probed* at the right time, e.g., someone tells you to count the potholes, then this information will appear to enter your conscious mind. According to Dennett, what this actually means is that the probe precipitates a cascade of activity that *promotes* some neural computational agent processing information that is normally ignored to a position of *disproportionate influence*. Whereas the activity of most neural computational agents dies out very quickly and has no further effect on the behaviour of the whole system (the person), the activity of some agents is amplified and has long-term effects on memory, speech and behaviour. *Which* agents have their activity amplified into long-term, lasting effects on the whole system varies and depends largely on context: on how and when the nervous system is probed.

The most versatile tool for initiating such probes and precipitating such amplifications of influence is language. Not only can other people trigger such amplifications in your brain by telling you to do things; you are constantly triggering such amplifications by talking to yourself. This constant verbal self-probing creates a kind of stream of consciousness: the sequence of computational agents the activity of which gets amplified into long-term effects on memory, further speech and behaviour. Though this sequence may consist in a motley collection of different agents succeeding each other, it appears as if it is the activity of just one agent: the self, in control of the operation. This is how the illusion of the Cartesian Theatre arises.

I shall have much more to say about Dennett's proposal in chapter 4. However, it should already be apparent why he calls the model the fame in the brain model. The stream of consciousness is the sequence of neural computational agents that happen to achieve fame in the brain, i.e., disproportionate influence on the brain's future activity. *Which* computational agents achieve this status is to a large degree accidental, or contingent on various contextual factors, such as which other computational agents have previously had such status, and the environment in which the overall system, i.e., the person, finds itself.

It is instructive to consider a sociopolitical metaphor in order to understand Dennett's proposal. Consider the sequence of presidential administrations in United States history. It is easy to succumb to the illusion that essentially the same group has been in charge of the United States since its inception.[11] However, there is another way of understanding this history. Each administration is the result of numerous political processes going on in parallel, all over the country: coalitions forming, competing or cooperating with each other, etc. In addition, there are unpredictable contextual factors, like events going on in the rest of the world. This complex tumult of parallel processes is interrupted by a probe every four years – a general election – the result of which is the promotion of one coalition to disproportionate though temporary influence over the country. The coalition that happens to be so promoted is *one of* the contextual factors that constrains which coalition gets promoted as a result of the *next* probe, the next general election, but there are many other contextual factors and no particular coalition is guaranteed to be in charge all the time. Looking back, as historians, we can discern a certain pattern in the sequence of coalitions that happen to have achieved the status of presidential administrations. And, from this perspective, the members of this sequence look to have a lot in common, almost as if there has been one coalition in charge all of the time. But this order and continuity is something of an illusion that emerges from the behind-the-scenes tumult that characterizes the democratic process.[12]

The brain pulls off a similar trick, according to Dennett. Probes, some initiated by the neural computational agents that happen to be temporarily influential in the brain, others coming from the environment, lead to amplification of the activity of other computational agents and, thereby, to a disproportionate increase in their influence on future activity by the whole system. Retrospectively, the sequence of such temporary amplifications of influence looks to have a certain order – as if there has been just one agent in charge all of the time. But this is an illusion.

Dennett's key idea is that consciousness is not some kind of place or special medium of representation in the brain, such that once information enters this 'charmed circle', it is guaranteed to be conscious, and before it enters, it is guaranteed not to be conscious. This way of thinking is an artefact of the Cartesian Theatre Model. On Dennett's model, the same information in the brain, processed by the same computational agent, in the same 'place', may at one time be conscious, and at another time be unconscious, depending on how the brain is being probed in the context in which the person finds themselves.

According to Dennett, the idea that there is a 'charmed circle' of consciousness in the brain is based on what his teacher, Gilbert Ryle, calls a 'category-mistake' (Ryle 1949, p. 17): a category appropriate to the *macroscopic* scales relating whole persons to their environments is *misapplied* to the *microscopic* scales relating events within individual brains (CE, pp. 107–108). In particular, the distinction between *observed* and *yet-to-be-observed* events, which makes perfect sense when applied to whole persons, is applied to events within individual brains. According to Dennett, these categories make no sense when applied to events *within* individual brains because they imply an intelligent, conscious homunculus: an observer *inside the brain*, relative to which some events count as observed, and others as yet-to-be-observed.

In contrast, if Dennett's fame in the brain model of consciousness is correct, then there is no general answer to the question of whether some information has entered the charmed circle of consciousness or not. Any information being processed by any of the myriad, continually active parallel processes in the brain is potentially conscious; it all depends on how and when the brain is probed, e.g., what the experimental subject is told to do or say under what circumstances. In one context, one kind of probe might precipitate a cascade of brain activity that amplifies the information being processed by one area of the brain, promoting it to influential status. In another context, the same probe might not have this effect, and a different probe might promote a different stream of information processing to influential status. Furthermore, consciousness comes in degrees: information is conscious to the degree that it has subsequent influence on processing in the brain and, consequently, overt behaviour. Therefore nothing is absolutely conscious or unconscious; rather, there are degrees of consciousness corresponding to the degree to which some stream of information processing has influence on overall brain activity and consequent behaviour (SD, pp. 170–1).

The most important kind of influence consists in the control of *verbal* behaviour because subjects hear themselves talk, so such influence feeds back into the brain, amplifying influence even more.[13] This explains why Dennett claims that heterophenomenology captures all the data that needs explaining by a theory of consciousness. Heterophenomenology is anchored in subjects' verbal reports about how things appear to them. As such, it gives theorists a window on which information processing streams are promoted to influential status in certain contexts, and on which information processing streams are likely to be promoted in the future, given the feedback effects of a subject's hearing their own verbal reports.

The method of heterophenomenology assumes that the subject is authoritative about what they *believe* goes on in their mind, and constructs a hypothetical world based on their reports. Initially, this world must be hypothetical, since to grant a subject unchallenged authority about what is *actually* happening in their mind is to abandon science, with its canons of intersubjective verifiability. If we then look at how the brain actually processes information, we find that a lot of what the subject thinks goes on in their mind does not. Our only option is to explain why they *think* their mind is a Cartesian Theatre. Once this is accomplished, the explanatory project ends: we have explained all of the causes and effects of their judgements about their conscious mind.

Dennett's many antagonists are not satisfied by this. According to them, the theory leaves out the most important part: what these judgements are about, qualia, or the intrinsic features of experience. They appeal to what appears to be a common-sense distinction: the difference between a person's *judgement* or *report* of how things appear and how things *really* appear. Surely when you judge that the water has turned hotter, there are two things going on in your mind: the judgement and the appearance of water turning hotter. Heterophenomenology only captures the *effects* of neural processes on subjects' first-person reports. Qualia are supposed to be *intrinsic* properties of neural processes that such judgements are about; so, they exist independently of any such effects. Thus, they cannot be captured by heterophenomenology. Everything that Dennett says about human brains is true of zombie brains: language-mediated self-probing can lead to amplification and promotion of certain neural processes, to disproportionate influence on subsequent neural activity and behaviour, in zombies as much as in human beings. But, goes this line of objection, zombies are nonetheless unconscious, because their neural processes do not have qualia.

At this point, the debate degenerates into what some have called table thumping. Dennett throws up his hands: he claims that qualia, so conceived, do not exist (Dennett 1988; SD, p. 101). These are supposed to be intrinsic properties of neural states that make no scientifically detectable difference, not even to persons' judgements about their own conscious states![14] Since qualia make no scientifically detectable difference, they should be eliminated by Ockham's Razor, the methodological principle that scientific theories should not multiply entities beyond necessity (CE, p. 134). With qualia eliminated, the distinction between conscious persons and their zombie duplicates breaks down: according to Dennett, despite appearances, either we are all zombies or zombies are impossible (CE, pp. 405–6; SD, p. 150). Dennett's antagonists are just as incredulous about his proposal as he is about theirs: to them the existence of qualia is undeniable, and Dennett's arguments lead to the absurd conclusion that we are, in fact, zombies, that there is nothing it is like to be us.

Loose ends

We have seen some of the ways in which Dennett's theory accommodates the intuitions that support the Cartesian Theatre, while rejecting this model in favour of a more scientifically informed theory of consciousness. The conscious self that constitutes the audience in the Cartesian Theatre is an illusion. The 'stream of consciousness' that actually constitutes the self is nothing but a motley sequence of neurocomputational agents that happen, for various contingent reasons, to achieve disproportionate, though temporary, influence on the overall activity of the nervous system and, consequently, on a person's public behaviour, and especially speech. Dennett accommodates the first-person authority that subjects appear to have regarding the nature of their conscious states by incorporating this as a central assumption of heterophenomenology, his third-person method for specifying the data of consciousness. Anything a subject judges to be true of their conscious experience is assumed to be true of a hypothetical world that Dennett calls the subject's 'heterophenomenological world,' i.e., what the subject takes their conscious mind to be like. However, there is no guarantee that this is what their conscious mind is *really* like: if consciousness is to be studied scientifically, then any theory of consciousness, including the subject's theory of their own consciousness, must be publicly verifiable.

Those features of a subject's heterophenomenological world that do not correspond to what science discovers about their real mind–brain must be explained: why does the brain create such powerful illusions? We have discussed Dennett's explanation of the illusion of the self, and his accommodation of the authority of the subject. But other features remain unexplained. Why is conscious experience so difficult to express in language, i.e., why does it seem ineffable? What are we to make of the thought experiment involving Mary, the colour-blind neuroscientist? What explains our intuition that consciousness is something special and rare in the natural world, and how did this phenomenon evolve, given that, presumably, there was a time when nothing was conscious? Finally, how does Dennett's theory accommodate non-human consciousness, given the important role that verbal behaviour plays in his theory? Chapter 4 endeavours to answer these questions.

The Joycean machine

Chapter Four

Preamble

According to Dennett, the conscious self is a kind of illusion. Rather than a bureaucracy governed by an all-powerful central executive, the mind–brain is a tumult of specialist neurocomputational agents, each performing limited tasks with limited access to information. The conscious mind consists of a sequence of (coalitions of) such agents that are promoted to disproportionate influence on overall brain activity and behaviour, thanks to amplification by certain attention-grabbing stimuli, like verbal self-stimulation. Dennett calls this sequence the 'Joycean machine' (CE, p. 214), after James Joyce, the author who pioneered stream of consciousness prose. The illusion that there is a conscious self in the brain, first attending to one bit of information, then to another, is caused by this Joycean machine.

Dennett understands the Joycean machine in terms of a metaphor drawn from computer science: it is a virtual machine running on the hardware of the brain. A virtual machine is a machine that is *simulated* on an actual computer, rather like virtual reality. Any general purpose computer, for example, the standard desktop personal computer, can implement numerous virtual machines. General purpose computers all share the same architecture: the 'Von Neumann Architecture', designed by John von Neumann in the 1950s. This architecture consists of a capacious, highly reliable memory that stores data (the standard computer's hard drive), and a limited capacity workspace (the standard computer's RAM), where a limited number of simple operations[1] are applied, by a central processor (the standard computer's CPU), to information imported from the memory. Von Neumann's architecture is inspired by the Turing Machine, Alan Turing's abstract, mathematical model of a mechanism capable of solving any problem that can be solved by following a series of simple steps, or an *algorithm*.[2] This is why von Neumann machines can implement different virtual machines: each virtual machine consists in a set of algorithmically solvable problems and, because von Neumann machines embody Turing Machines, they are able to solve such problems. Desktop computers can simulate word processors, spread sheets, chess and other games, etc., *because* they are von Neumann machines. Any software that your computer runs specifies a virtual machine, by 'telling' your computer the series of steps it must follow in order to implement the algorithms that define the virtual machine.

Because von Neumann machines are so versatile, they can implement a wide range of virtual machines. In fact, they can even implement virtual machines that are structurally very different from von Neumann machines. For example, they can simulate connectionist models of the brain (Rumelhart *et al.* 1986). Like the brain, these models process large amounts of information *in parallel*. Rather than one central processing unit where information from memory is brought and submitted to a *series* of simple operations, parallel processing computers, like the brain and connectionist models, consist of numerous processors processing different information at the same time. But von Neumann machines can simulate such parallel machines: they simply take all the information that is supposed to be processed simultaneously by different processors in a parallel machine, and process it very rapidly, in a single sequence. In this way, a von Neumann machine can implement a virtual parallel computer.

Dennett's theory is that human consciousness arises when the human brain does the reverse: the massively parallel hardware of the human brain implements a virtual von Neumann machine. In the brain, millions of limited computational agents process information in parallel. But consciousness resembles a serial, von Neumann machine:[3] in the stream of consciousness, the self appears to consider one bit of information at a time. Somehow, the massively parallel architecture of the human brain has managed to simulate a von Neumann machine: the stream of consciousness is nothing other than a virtual Joycean machine running on the brain. How does the brain accomplish this? By engaging in the kind of verbal self-stimulation – the kind of talking to oneself – that I discussed in chapter 3. Language is a serial medium: you can only talk about one thing at a time. When one talks to oneself, one imposes this serial discipline on the parallel architecture of the brain. This virtual Joycean machine is a kind of user illusion that conceals the real work of the brain, rather like desktop user interfaces of standard software conceal the complex operations taking place in a standard computer's hardware (CE, pp. 214–18).

This is Dennett's basic model of the conscious mind, and it raises a host of questions. First, how did a brain capable of implementing a virtual Joycean machine evolve? Second, if human consciousness is nothing but a virtual Joycean machine running on the brain, then why does it seem so special? After all, desktop computers are von Neumann Machines, but they are not conscious. Third, if the conscious self is nothing but an illusion, then how can anything matter? How can things have value? Fourth, what about all the loose ends left dangling in chapter 3? Why are conscious experiences ineffable? Why does Mary appear to learn something when she is let out of her black and white room? What kind of consciousness is possible for persons and animals that cannot use human language? This chapter explores Dennett's answers to these questions.

The evolution of the Joycean machine

Prior to the emergence of life on this planet, there was no consciousness here. There were no selves and there were no actions or reasons for actions. Things just happened. Boulders were caused to topple from mountainsides; liquids were caused to boil; volcanoes were caused to erupt; but nothing was done for a reason, or for a purpose. How did purposes, reasons, selves and consciousness emerge from such a mindless environment? Dennett proposes an evolutionary story that aims to answer this question. Such stories raise thorny methodological issues. How can we possibly know whether such a story is true? We cannot travel back in time to verify it. What constraints are there on the construction of such narratives? Some critics worry that anything goes in such narratives, and lampoon them as 'just-so stories'.[4] However, even if we will never know in detail how life and mind evolved on the planet, constructing plausible narratives that explain this is hardly idle and without constraints. There must be some account of how life, mind and consciousness evolved. We know for a fact that there was a time when these phenomena were absent from the earth, and we know for a fact that they are present now. Somehow, this gap was bridged. If one accepts science, and therefore foregoes appeals to miraculous intervention, then any account of how this gap was bridged must be constrained by our scientific understanding of nature. And we know enough from fossil records, the nature of today's life forms, and our understanding of physically possible processes, to put substantial constraints on our speculations about how the gap was bridged. Dennett's story, though undoubtedly wrong about many details, is a responsible attempt to explain the evolution of consciousness, by constructing a *plausible* narrative, i.e., a narrative constrained by what we know, from science, about how the world works.

According to Dennett, the first step in the evolution of consciousness was the emergence of *reasons* from a world of mere *causes*. Once there were things with *interests* on the scene, there were reasons for them to do things. How might things with interests have emerged? According to Dennett, once there are things that count as *replicators*, it makes sense to infer that there are interests. A replicator is any structure that can make copies of itself. Extremely rudimentary life-forms qualify as replicators. The earliest ones were probably far simpler even than viruses, today's simplest biological replicators. Once such entities were floating around in the primordial soup, we can infer that there were already reasons: reasons for the replicators to do some things rather than others. This is because replicators have goals or purposes. At the most basic level, their goal is to replicate. Anything that serves this goal for a replicator counts as advancing its interests. Since the replicator aims to replicate, it has a reason to do anything that contributes to this goal.[5]

There are two basic strategies that replicators have evolved to replicate more efficiently. In a harsh environment, consisting largely of other replicators with which a replicator competes for scarce resources necessary for replication, it pays either to stay put and grow a lot of 'armour', or to move around in an intelligent manner. The first strategy characterizes most plant life. Plants rely on sturdy barriers to resist environmental dangers. The second strategy characterizes animal life. Animals avoid danger and acquire what they need to survive and reproduce by *moving*. In order to move, one needs a control system – something that controls behavioural responses efficiently and intelligently. This is why animals have nervous systems and plants do not.

The first animals had very rudimentary nervous systems. A current-day example of such an animal is the sea squirt: it uses its brain only to find a safe nook under some rock, where it can reproduce. Once it finds an appropriate location, it does not need its brain anymore, so it eats it![6] Such rudimentary nervous systems hardly count as control systems at all. The behaviours they trigger resemble reflexes. However, under pressure from natural selection, more sophisticated control systems are likely to evolve. In an environment of constant competition for scarce resources, replicators with slightly more sophisticated nervous systems, capable of controlling a wider range of behavioural response, and dedicated to accomplishing more goals, are bound to have an advantage. The results of millions of years of such dynamics are animals with *diversified* nervous systems: brains consisting of different specialist components dedicated to accomplishing different tasks, principally, feeding, fleeing, fighting and reproducing (CE, p. 188).

Animals with such nervous systems do everything on autopilot. The environment triggers the activation of an appropriate specialist component that controls the animal's behaviour in a very stereotyped manner, rather like driving to work along a familiar route without paying any attention. However, there is some evidence that even fairly primitive animals have evolved, in addition, an orienting response. When some potentially significant yet hard to classify stimulus is detected, this triggers an 'all hands on deck' signal, activating all of the brain's specialist components simultaneously, and creating a temporary 'global' workspace, where any information available to any component can be brought to bear on classifying and responding to the stimulus. Dennett argues that this orienting response, which underlies animals' capacity for *vigilance*, is an early, primitive precursor to human consciousness (CE, p. 180).

Once such a capacity developed, individuals that had more *endogenous* control over triggering the orienting response would have an advantage. That is, individuals that could activate the orienting response and remain vigilant *even in the absence* of some potentially significant yet hard to classify stimulus, would likely evolve, for the following reason: it pays to be informed about one's environment. Such creatures would have the capacity to acquire and store information about the environment for future use, even in the absence of any occurrent need for it. Dennett calls such inveterately curious creatures 'informavores', because of their constant hunger for information (CE, p. 181). Current mammalian species all qualify as informavores, to different degrees, with human beings and our nearest cousins, the great apes, at the extreme end of this spectrum.

Among the information in which informavores are interested is information about *regularities* in the environment. The best way to control behaviour efficiently and intelligently is to *anticipate* the future (CE, p. 177). If one knows where prey or predators or mates or offspring will be, then one can prepare oneself appropriately. The most stable regularities in the environment can be discovered through genetic selection. Individuals whose brains are better tuned to stable regularities have a reproductive advantage over individuals whose brains are not as well tuned. However, as species interact with increasingly chaotic environments, natural selection becomes a very inefficient means for constructing brains capable of tracking important regularities. Natural selection gives individuals the capacities of their parents, transmitted with their genes. But if the regularities relevant to survival are so unstable that they change in a small number of generations, then brains will not be appropriately wired to deal with new regularities, unless they are lucky enough to be the products of appropriate genetic mutations – an extremely unlikely possibility. As a result, individuals whose brains are capable of *learning* the regularities that happen to be relevant in their lifetimes have an enormous advantage. This led to selection for *phenotypic plasticity*: the capacity of an individual to adapt, within its lifetime, to contingent regularities in its environment. For example, squirrels do not necessarily hunt for nuts where their parents did. They can learn to find nuts in new locations.

According to Dennett, the evolution of phenotypic plasticity led to a qualitatively different type of evolution. Increases in nervous system complexity were no longer merely the result of differential reproduction of genes. Increases in intelligence did not have to await lucky mutations that improved some individual's capacities over those of its parents. A similar process now took place *within* the nervous systems of individuals. Different populations of neural structures and processes now competed for control of individual behaviour, and the fittest of these, i.e., those that best tracked local regularities and controlled intelligent responses, gained control of individual behaviour.

Higher mammals, and especially our primate cousins, are products of this new, qualitatively different type of evolution that incorporates phenotypic plasticity. So were our primate ancestors. These species are incredibly efficient at satisfying their biological goals. They show impressive flexibility and sensitivity to environmental contingencies. In many respects, their intelligence matches our own; in fact, we share many of the same neural capacities. Dennett characterizes the cognitive life of pre-human informavores in the following way:

> [O]ur hypothetical primate ancestor ... [was] an animal capable of learning new tricks, and almost continually vigilant and sensitive to novelty, but with a 'short-attention span' and a tendency to have attention 'captured' by distracting environmental features. No long-term projects for this animal, at least not novel projects ...

> (CE, p. 189)

This cognitive profile sets the stage for the final step in the evolution of human consciousness. Dennett continues: 'Onto this substrate nervous system we now want to imagine building a more human mind, with something like a "stream of consciousness" capable of sustaining the sophisticated sorts of "trains of thought" on which human civilization apparently depends' (CE, p. 189).

The cognitive capacities of higher mammals are products of two qualitatively different kinds of evolution. First, like the rest of the living world, they are products of natural selection for better genes. This is a relatively slow form of selection because it relies on differential reproduction and lucky mutations alone; generations pass between innovations. Second, because of their extreme phenotypic plasticity, the cognitive capacities of higher mammals are also products of selection for better neural control systems within the lifetimes of individuals. According to Dennett, human consciousness is the product of these two kinds of evolution, together with yet a third, qualitatively different kind: cultural evolution. Alone among current species, humans *rely* on learning culturally transmitted traditions in order to flourish. Many species exhibit behaviour that is socially transmitted, and some may even be capable of rudimentary imitation (Boesch 1991). However, no other species relies on cultural transmission of complex suites of skills that no individual could possibly acquire on its own (Boyd and Richerson 1996; Tomasello *et al.* 1993).

As Dennett points out, our virtuosity at learning from each other, through imitation, pedagogy, reading, etc., constitutes a quantum leap in our capacity to intelligently adapt to the environment (CE, pp. 193, 208; FE, p. 173). Unlike other creatures, we do not need to constantly reinvent the wheel. Culture preserves the hard-won accomplishments of previous generations, transmits them to future generations, and permits their elaboration by future generations. In this way, novices can quickly acquire complex skills that have been pre-tested and, at the same time, improve upon them. These innovations accumulate and, eventually, skills that no individual could discover on their own are acquired through social learning.[7] Psychologists term such dynamics the 'ratchet effect' (Tomasello *et al.* 1993), or 'cumulative cultural evolution' (Boyd and Richerson 1996). The idea is that sophisticated cultural learning enables our species to 'ratchet up' our cognitive skills, in a spiral of improvement.

Given the importance of cultural learning in human evolution, our minds, unlike those of other animals, are largely products of culture. This fact leads Dennett and others to defend a specific model of cultural evolution: the memetic model. The idea, first proposed by Dawkins (1976), is that ideas passed down through culture, called 'memes', behave much like genes passed down through biological reproduction. Just as the science of genetics studies the proliferation of different genes in different biological environments, memetics is supposed to study the proliferation of memes in different cultural environments. According to Dawkins (1976) and Dennett (CE, p. 202), this is more than a metaphor: memes, like genes, are *replicators*. Just as genes rely on the survival and reproductive success of individual organisms to survive and replicate, memes rely on individual human brains to survive and replicate. Memes survive and replicate when they are remembered and communicated by individual human minds. They are rather like viruses of the mind. Human minds are infected by memes through communication with other human minds. These memes live, grow and mutate in individual minds, and then are transmitted again. Any skill or set of information that catches on with human beings counts as a meme. Good examples are catchy songs, technologies, stories, recipes and religious beliefs.[8] Such memes are not always beneficial to us. Sometimes pernicious memes spread, e.g., the body-image driving anorexia,[9] much like computer viruses spread through the Internet.

How is all of this related to the evolution of human consciousness? Perhaps the most important meme of all is the meme for human language. Many if not most memes are transmitted through language: whenever we talk to each other, memes are transmitted. According to Dennett, a relatively rudimentary language used by our precursors for social transmission of information, could easily have evolved into a Joycean virtual machine, used by the brain to control thought.

As Dennett points out, our primate precursors had solved all the important *behavioural* control problems: they were experts at fulfiling their biological imperatives in efficient and flexible ways; they knew what to *do* next. However, the structure of their cognitive capacities spawned a higher-level control problem: what to think about next (CE, p. 222). Because they were informavores, constantly vigilant, flooded with multi-modal information triggering countless neurocomputational agents simultaneously, they had trouble organizing and structuring their cognitive processing. Their minds consisted of a near chaotic tumult of computational agents competing for control of behaviour. They needed some way of imposing control on this chaos: some way of resolving disputes between competing processes, and coordinating *sequences* of control to make coherent, long-term behaviour possible. According to Dennett, this capacity emerged when our precursors learned how to talk to themselves.

The capacity to talk to oneself may have emerged as a lucky by-product of talking to others, something our precursors could presumably do, once sophisticated cultural learning was on the scene. In order for a practice of sharing information through vocal communication to emerge in a population, there must be *reciprocity*: individuals must be willing to share useful information when asked, if they expect to receive useful information when they ask for it. Thus, any population that shares information in this way must consist of individuals capable of *both* responding to queries and making queries. The idea is that when one individual is working on some task and cannot access relevant information, they automatically vocalize a query. Upon hearing this, another individual, if they happen to have access to the relevant information, automatically responds. But the roles can always be reversed; this is guaranteed by reciprocity. Now, given such a population, Dennett asks us to imagine the following scenario: an individual is working on some task alone. They cannot access relevant information, because it is locked away in some specialist neural subsystem to which the currently active subsystem has no access. Given their habit of asking others for information that they cannot access themselves, they automatically voice a query, but because they are members of a population in which individuals automatically answer such queries if they hear them, upon hearing their own query, they automatically vocalize the answer: the information for which their brain has no *internal* prompt, is triggered by their own mechanism of vocal response, and they hear themselves respond to their own query with the information they lack.

As Dennett puts it,

> [P]ushing some information through one's ears and auditory system may well happen to stimulate just the sorts of connections one is seeking, may trip just the right associative mechanisms, tease just the right mental morsel to the tip of one's tongue. One can then say it, hear oneself say it, and thus get the answer one was hoping for.
>
> (CE, p. 196)

Dennett thinks of this as the installation of a 'virtual wire' (CE, p. 196) in the brain. Two subsystems that are not neurally connected become connected through self-directed speech. Language becomes a way of *controlling the flow of information* within the brain. Because this is precisely the capacity that, according to Dennett, our precursors lacked and sorely needed, the habit of talking to oneself constituted a 'good trick' that quickly spread through the population via cultural transmission (CE, pp. 196–7). At the same time it was elaborated: it became a kind of sophisticated, silent, self-directed speech in which human beings constantly engaged, to control the tumult of parallel processing in their brains. The Joycean machine had been installed!

The self as centre of narrative gravity

Dennett explains his theory of the conscious self with three distinct yet closely related metaphors. As we saw in chapter 3, the conscious self can be understood in terms of a political metaphor: though there appears to be one all-powerful agent in charge of the mind–brain, it is actually an orderly sequence of (coalitions of) different computational agents, each limited in its capacities and access to information, rather like the sequence of presidential administrations in United States history. This same phenomenon can also be understood in terms of a metaphor drawn from computer science: the conscious self is a 'von Neumannesque' virtual machine (CE, p. 210) running on the massively parallel hardware of the brain. Finally, the self can be understood in terms of a biological metaphor: human brains develop conscious selves when they are parasitized by memes, transmitted largely through language, and promoted to disproportionate influence over the control of information in the brain through self-directed speech. Although slightly confusing, this mix of metaphors articulates a coherent and highly original model of the conscious self.

However, it is bound to leave many unsatisfied. There remains the residual feeling that the conscious self, for all of Dennett's vivid metaphors, is, ultimately, a mere illusion; it is not anything *real* in the brain. There is no one really in charge in there, just as there is no single political entity that has ruled the United States throughout history, and just as computers are not really typewriters when they run word processing software. This worry comes to the fore when Dennett discusses the role of memes in creating the conscious self. His view that the brain develops a self when it is parasitized by memes via mechanisms of cultural transmission, like language, encourages a vision of the mind as invaded by foreign agents against which it must struggle. However, Dennett argues that this is the wrong way to think of it. What the conscious self *is*, who *we* are, is *determined* by the memes that control our brains. We do not make memes, nor do we choose to accept certain memes and reject others. Rather, memes make us: they transform our brains into environments hospitable to further memes. As Dennett puts it, on this view 'a scholar is just a library's way of making another library' (CE, p. 202). But, if our behaviour is exclusively the product of the massively parallel processing of our brains, controlled by memes invading from the ambient culture, what work is left for the conscious self?

Dennett responds to this question by appeal to yet another concept first proposed by Dawkins (1982): the extended phenotype. Classically, biologists understand a species' phenotype as the physical expression of its genotype in proteins and other substances that *compose the bodies* of individuals of the species.

However, Dawkins argues that, in many species, the phenotype *extends* to incorporate stable objects in the species' environment that are not parts of the bodies of individual members of the species. For example, spiders spin webs. Though these are produced by organs within the spider's body, they are not literally parts of the spider's body. However, they are as crucial to the biological success of the spider as any part of its body: they are *extensions* of the spider phenotype. The phenomenon is even more pronounced in the Australian Bower Bird. The male Australian Bower Bird builds 'bowers', or nests in which to mate, to impress females. The 'flashiest' bowers are the most attractive, and males often incorporate human artefacts, like bottle caps and beads, into their designs. There is a default expectation of material in the environment, which individuals can automatically incorporate into a biologically crucial behaviour. According to Dennett, the self constructed by normal human brains is part of the extended human phenotype: human brains are born with the default expectation that their environment will contain millions of mostly word-borne memes, which they can automatically 'weave' into a narrative, a coherent sequence, that defines the self.

Thus, according to Dennett, the conscious self is a *centre of narrative gravity*. Like centres of physical gravity, the self is not something concrete. Because centres of physical gravity are abstract, mathematical points, no actual, spatially extended part of a physical object constitutes its centre of gravity. Similarly, no actual, spatially extended part of a human brain constitutes its centre of narrative gravity. The brain consists of numerous, dedicated and limited computational agents, none of which has the powers that we take conscious selves to have. For this reason, the centre of narrative gravity is an *abstraction*: it is something we must assume exists when we interpret the narrative of memes spun by an individual brain as issuing from a *narrator*. No such author actually exists *within the brain*: the narrator is an illusion created by the cooperative activity of numerous dedicated and limited computational agents promoted to temporary and disproportionate influence by amplifying mechanisms like self-directed speech.

However, according to Dennett, this does not mean that the centre of narrative gravity is not useful, or important, or real. Just as centres of physical gravity are useful and important to understanding how physical objects behave, centres of narrative gravity are useful and important to understanding how human brains work. For this reason, such objects, though abstract, should nonetheless count as *real*.[10] They make a real difference to our ability to explain the behaviour of concrete objects. And, in the case of the centre of narrative gravity, there is an even more important function. Since the brain's ability to control itself depends largely on how it understands itself, and understanding itself as a centre of narrative gravity is so useful, this understanding makes a real difference to the brain's capacity to control itself. By thinking of themselves as centres of narrative gravity, human brains accomplish a biologically pressing task: higher level, cognitive control. As Dennett points out, this constitutes 'a major alteration in the competence' of the brain (CE, p. 209). The conscious self's status as an abstraction, or a fiction, far from a diminution, explains its glory: it is not just any fiction, argues Dennett; it is a 'magnificent fiction' (CE, p. 429).

Although this goes some way towards resuscitating the importance of the conscious self, in the wake of Dennett's theory, it is still not clear how the self as centre of narrative gravity is supposed to perform the jobs of the manifest concept of the self. According to the manifest image, the self is capable of freely choosing courses of action. The notion of moral responsibility hinges on this: as Dennett himself puts it, the self is where the buck stops (CE, p. 32). However, if the self is really just a useful abstraction created when memes absorbed from the ambient culture control a tumult of limited computational agents, in what sense is anyone really free to choose otherwise than they do, and in what sense is anyone really morally responsible for what they do? A detailed answer to these questions must await chapter 5, where I explain Dennett's account of the third major component of the manifest image of persons: freedom and responsibility.

Another job that the manifest image reserves for the conscious self is the capacity to truly appreciate and value certain objects and states. We may someday build a machine capable of accurately rating the value of wine vintages, but will such a machine be *truly* capable of appreciating the taste of wine, in the way that conscious human selves are? Human consciousness has a strong *affective* component. Consciousness not only informs us of the world, it automatically *evaluates* this information: we see things as pleasant or unpleasant, joyful or sorrowful, painful or pleasurable. According to Dennett, his theory can perfectly well accommodate this aspect of the conscious self. Consciousness, for Dennett, consists in those neural processes that are amplified and promoted to disproportionate influence on subsequent processing and behaviour. The hard question for a science of consciousness is: 'And then what happens?' (SD, p. 138). Any answer to this must specify, precisely and thoroughly, in what this subsequent processing and behaviour consists. According to Dennett, this subsequent processing inevitably involves a strong evaluative component:

> Our discriminative states are not just discriminable; they have the power to provoke preferences in us. Given choices between them, we are not indifferent, but these preferences are themselves subtle, variable, and highly dependent on other conditions. There is a time for chocolate and a time for cheese, a time for blue and a time for yellow. In short ... many if not all of our discriminative states have what might be called a dimension of affective valence. We care which states we are in, and this caring is reflected in our dispositions to change state.

> (SD, p. 175)

This, according to Dennett, should not surprise us, given the evolutionary pedigree of our conscious, sensory states. The computational agents responsible for them are descendants of more primitive mechanisms that acted as 'warners and beckoners' rather than 'disinterested reporters' (CE, p. 384). They functioned to warn us against things that were bad for us, and to beckon us towards things that were good for us. So it is no surprise that conscious states are automatically evaluative. Thus, the appreciation made possible by conscious awareness, according to Dennett, succumbs to exactly the kind of explanatory treatment recommended by his model: once we specify clearly and thoroughly in what the disproportionate influence of computational agents promoted to conscious status consists, we should understand their role in the capacity to *truly* appreciate and value.

But there is another worry about Dennett's model: if consciousness is the simulation of a von Neumannesque Joycean machine on the parallel architecture of the brain, then why are real von Neumann machines, like standard desktop computers, not conscious? Dennett responds that there is something about the *way* in which our brains implement a virtual von Neumannesque machine that explains this difference:

> The von Neumann machine, by being wired up from the outset that way, with maximally efficient informational links, didn't have to become the object of its own elaborate perceptual systems. The workings of the Joycean machine, on the other hand, are just as 'visible' and 'audible' to it as any of the things in the external world that it is designed to perceive – for the simple reason that they have much the same perceptual machinery focused on them.

(CE, pp. 225–6)

The Joycean machine consists in the sequence of information processing amplified to disproportionate status *largely through self-stimulation*, that is, information fed back into the brain *through the senses* by self-directed activity, like speech. Consequently, this information is treated in the same way as the senses treat information provided by the environment. It is in this that much of the ineffability and consequent apparent mystery of consciousness consist. So, the plausibility of Dennett's proposal depends, to a large degree, on his account of the ineffability of sensory information. I turn to this and other 'loose ends' next.

Tying up loose ends

In the previous section, I discussed Dennett's responses to some of the more obvious problems that arise for his theory of consciousness. Here, I turn to three specific problems that were raised in chapter 3: the ineffability of experience, what Mary the colour-blind neuroscientist learns and non-human consciousness.[11]

The ineffability of conscious experience consists in its inexpressibility: it seems impossible to convey in words the conscious experience of the colour red, for example, to a person who has never experienced it. Much of the apparent mystery of consciousness derives from this fact. As we saw above, Dennett argues that what distinguishes the conscious von Neumannesque virtual machine run on the human brain, from real, unconscious von Neumann machines, such as desktop computers, is the involvement of our *senses*. Human brains implement von Neumannesque virtual machines when they feed information back through the senses through various kinds of self-stimulation. But the information provided by the senses is the best example of ineffable information: the experience of colours, tastes and smells is notoriously difficult to express. So, it is consistent with Dennett's theory to claim that much of what makes consciousness seem so special is the apparent ineffability of sensory information. Dennett agrees that sensory information is *apparently* ineffable, but he does not think this at all mysterious: he seeks to explain this fact in scientific terms.

The 'flagship' examples of ineffable, sensory, conscious states are experiences of colour. Colour has been a notoriously puzzling concept for philosophers since the rise of modern science. According to the manifest image, colours exist outside our minds, as *simple* properties of the surfaces of objects. However, there is no simple, scientifically detectable property of object surfaces that matches the manifest concept of colour. Object surfaces that reflect only wavelengths of light from the 'red' part of the spectrum do not always appear red to normal human observers. It all depends on the viewing conditions: the ambient light, the other objects in the scene, etc. Also, in some viewing conditions, objects that reflect wavelengths of light from the 'non-red' part of the spectrum appear red to normal observers. If one looks at all objects that normal human observers call 'red' – sunsets, apples, old Soviet flags, Cincinnati Reds baseball caps, oranges at dusk – they appear to have nothing objective, nothing scientifically detectable, in common. All they have in common is the fact that humans call all such objects 'red'. This leads some philosophers and scientists to endorse a projectivist theory of colour: contrary to the manifest image, colour is not a property existing outside our minds, in the surfaces of objects; rather, it is *projected* by our minds onto objects.

Dennett cannot endorse projectivism. If colours are projected onto objects from within our minds, then there must be some non-physical Cartesian Theatre containing them, since they certainly do not exist in our brains. Since Dennett rejects the Cartesian Theatre, he must reject projectivism. According to Dennett, the manifest concept of colour has one thing right: colours do exist in objects, outside of our minds. However, it is wrong in another respect: colours are not *simple* properties of objects. They are incredibly complex, gerrymandered properties – too complex to *quickly and easily* express in words. However, because of the way the human brain evolved, these complex properties *appear* simple. This illusion gives rise to the intuition that conscious, sensory experiences are ineffable. They are *practically* ineffable because they represent properties that are too complex to describe quickly and easily. But this is not mysterious, once we understand why such properties should seem so simple to the sensory systems of the human brain.

According to Dennett, colours and animal visual systems *co-evolved.*[12] Co-evolution is a common phenomenon: whenever two biological traits affect each other's survival and reproduction, there is the potential for co-evolution. For example, lions and gazelles both run fast. This speed is the result of co-evolution: as lion speed increases, so must gazelle speed, and vice versa. Such reciprocal influence dramatically accelerates natural selection, yielding extreme traits, like lion and gazelle speed. Dennett argues that something similar happened with colours and colour-vision. The point of animal colour-vision is to quickly and efficiently detect significant stimuli: food, predators and mates, principally. So, for example, the fact that, to many animal visual systems, red pops out against a green background probably has something to do with the fact that many kinds of ripe fruit are red against a green background. But many of the significant stimuli that animal colour-vision detects themselves issue from *organisms* to which *animal* behaviour is significant. For example, many species of plant rely on animal consumption of their fruit in order to spread seeds. Such species of plant are likely to evolve in ways that make it more likely that animals will eat them. One way of doing this is to colour code: to evolve colours that are more easily detected by animal visual systems. This reciprocal influence yields a co-evolutionary dynamic: plants evolve colours that are more easily detectable by animal visual systems, and animal visual systems evolve so as to better detect these plants. The results of this are visual systems that are exquisitely tuned to detect very specific ranges of properties: animal visual systems and the colours of edible plants are 'made for each other'.

How does this explain the ineffability of colour experience? Because animal visual systems and colours co-evolved over eons, such that the former became extremely efficient detectors of the latter, no other means of representing colours is likely to match this efficiency. In particular, words will not be able to represent colours with anything like the efficiency that the visual system can represent them. The visual system was designed, by natural selection, to efficiently detect *just those idiosyncratic reflectance properties* that plants evolved to be more easily detected by the visual system. But since words were never designed for this function, they cannot possibly represent colours in the way the visual system does: this is why colours are *practically* ineffable. We could, in principle, express what all and only red things have in common using words, but never with the quickness, simplicity and efficiency of the visual system, which is tailor-made to represent colours.

Dennett further clarifies this proposal with the help of an analogy. In the 1950s, an American couple, Julius and Ethel Rosenberg, were convicted of spying for the Soviets. During their trial it came out that they had used a simple and ingenious system for making contact with foreign agents. They would rip a piece of cardboard off of a Jell-O box, and send it to the contact. Then, when it was time to meet, in order to verify that they were meeting the right person, they would produce one piece of the Jell-O box, and ask the contact to produce the other piece – the one they had mailed. The complex, jagged surfaces of these two pieces of cardboard were such that the only practical way of telling whether the piece produced by the contact was the right piece, was by putting the two pieces together to see whether they fit. Of course, it is possible to describe such surfaces using very long and complicated sentences. However, the only efficient and practical way of detecting the other piece of cardboard is by putting the two pieces together. The pieces of cardboard are made for each other, in the way that colours and colour vision are made for each other. It is for this reason that colours and other sensory properties appear ineffable. It is *practically* impossible to represent such properties in words, yet very easy for our sensory systems to represent them, because, due to co-evolution, sensory systems and sensory properties are made for each other.

This explanation of ineffability also goes some way towards explaining the intuition that Mary the colour-blind neuroscience genius learns something new when she first experiences colour. This is an example of what Dennett calls an 'intuition pump' (ER, p. 12). Intuition pumps are descriptions of hypothetical situations meant to 'pump our intuitions' – to provoke gut reactions. Appeal to such thought experiments is standard practice in philosophy.[13] In this case, we are supposed to imagine a situation that is, in practice, impossible: a person who knows everything that science could ever possibly tell us about the nervous system, and who acquired all of this knowledge in an environment completely devoid of colour. We are then asked for our intuitive response to the following question: upon her first exposure to colour, would this person learn something new? Typically, the intuition is that yes, the person would learn something new, namely, what colour looks like. This intuition appears to support the conclusion that what colour looks like is something distinct from what science can possibly tell us about how the nervous system works.

Dennett thinks that this and many other intuition pumps aimed at shielding human consciousness from standard scientific understanding are pernicious. In his words, they mistake 'a failure of imagination for an insight into necessity' (CE, p. 401). When you try to imagine a person who knows *everything that science could ever possibly tell us about the nervous system,* how can you be sure that you succeed? How can we imagine knowing this? And how can we come to conclusions about whether or not a person could know what it is like to see colours, given all of this information?

As Dennett points out, if Mary really knew *everything* about human nervous systems, including her own, then she would know exactly how her brain would react if ever confronted with a colour stimulus (CE, pp. 399–400). What would stop her from trying to put her brain into that state by some other means, while still in her black and white environment? In this way, could she not use her vast scientific knowledge of how the human nervous system works to discover what colours look like? Of course, her knowledge of how her brain would react is distinct from the actual reaction: Mary's use of *words* to *describe* the state her nervous system would enter upon exposure to red, for example, is not the same as her actually being in that state. But this gap is not mysterious if we accept Dennett's account of ineffability: it is impossible for words to convey exactly the same information about colour as colour vision, *in the same way*, because colour vision and colour co-evolved to be tailor-made for each other. The only way for Mary to represent colour in the way the visual system represents it is by throwing her own visual system into the appropriate state. This is why her theoretical, word-based knowledge of what happens in the nervous system, upon exposure to colour, is not equivalent to representing colour using her own visual system.

Thus, Dennett has plausible responses to many of the philosophical reasons that have been offered against scientific theories of consciousness, like his own. However, there is a more specific worry that arises, with particular urgency, for Dennett's theory. The capacity to talk, and especially to talk to oneself, plays an extremely important role in Dennett's theory. The Joycean machine is installed in the brain thanks largely to our habits of *verbal* self-stimulation. On Dennett's view, what makes some stream of information processing in the brain conscious is its amplification to disproportionate influence on overall brain activity, and such amplification is the result of, for the most part, self-directed speech. But there are many examples of creatures that common sense takes to be conscious even though they are incapable of any kind of speech or human language, let alone verbal auto-stimulation. Does Dennett's view imply that common sense is wrong on this point? Are cats, dogs, chimpanzees and humans who have not acquired language, *not conscious*?

According to Dennett, two questions must be distinguished. First, what does some cognitive system, e.g., an animal's nervous system, have to be able to do in order to count as conscious? Second, *how* do actual conscious nervous systems *accomplish* this function?[14] Dennett's answer to the first question is entirely neutral on the question of whether the language-deprived are conscious. His theory consists of:

1. the empirical hypothesis that our capacity to relive or rekindle contentful events is the most important feature of consciousness – indeed, as close to a defining feature of consciousness as we will ever find; and
2. the empirical hypothesis that this echoic capacity is due in large part to habits of self-stimulation that we pick up from human culture, that the Joycean machine in our brains is a virtual machine made of memes (SD, pp. 171–2).

As Dennett notes, these are 'independent claims' (SD, p. 172). In order to count as conscious, a cognitive system like an animal's nervous system must have means by which certain information processing streams can be promoted to disproportionate influence on the long-term, overall activity of the brain. This is what Dennett means by 'our capacity to relive or rekindle contentful events'. Elsewhere, he compares this to an 'echo chamber' (SD, p. 169): information rises to the status of consciousness in the brain when it 'echoes' through the brain for an extended period of time. *One* way of doing this is via habits of auto-stimulation, like the self-directed speech we acquire from culture. Some information processing streams are promoted to disproportionate influence because they keep feeding back into the brain thanks to obsessive, repetitive self-directed speech. But there may be other ways of accomplishing this.

If cognitive science discovers other mechanisms, in non-human animals for example, with such echo-making power, then his theory that consciousness is a largely language-based, culturally transmitted phenomenon will be undermined. But Dennett thinks this is unlikely. He argues that non-human animals do not have any need for the echo chamber of consciousness, and it is unlikely to be the by-product of anything else. To succeed in the wild, a species needs efficient and timely information processing; dwelling on or constantly replaying information of no use in the present wastes valuable time and energy. Somehow, writes Dennett, 'human beings got sidetracked. We developed a habit of "replaying events in our minds" over and over, and this habit, initially "wasteful" of time and energy, is very likely the source of our greatest talents' (SD, p. 169).

So, although Dennett's theory of what brains must do to be conscious leaves open the *possibility* that the language-deprived can be conscious, his empirical hunch is that the only way that evolution has discovered to accomplish this function is through self-directed speech, and other culturally transmitted habits of self-stimulation. Accordingly, it is Dennett's hunch that the language-deprived are not conscious – at least not in the way that language users are conscious. The language-deprived have no means by which information processing in the brain can 'echo', or be amplified to disproportionate influence on long-term, overall brain activity. Without this, what reason is there to call any bit of information processing, in a language-deprived brain, conscious? As Dennett puts it, 'What is *experiential* (as contrasted with what?) about a discrimination that is not globally accessible?' (SD, p. 143).

Dennett hesitates a bit on this issue (CE, p. 447). He does not come out and say that there is *not anything* it is like to be a bat, for example. On his theory, the question of whether some stream of information processing is conscious never has a simple yes or no answer. Consciousness is not guaranteed by entry into some 'charmed circle' in the brain; it comes in *degrees*. Information is conscious only to the degree that it has disproportionate influence on long-term, overall brain activity. So perhaps bats and other language-deprived creatures have minimal degrees of consciousness. But Dennett emphasizes how different this is from human consciousness: 'The sort of consciousness such animals enjoy is dramatically truncated, compared to ours. A bat, for instance, not only can't wonder whether it's Friday; it can't even wonder whether it's a bat' (CE, p. 447). And he argues that we do the language-deprived no favours if we refuse to appreciate what they are missing:

> [W]ithout a natural language, a deaf-mute's mind is terribly stunted ... One does not do deaf-mutes a favour by imagining that in the absence of language they enjoy all the mental delights we hearing human beings enjoy, and one does not do a favour to non-human animals by trying to obscure the available facts about the limitations of their minds.
>
> (CE, p. 448)

The way forward

The three central concepts of the manifest image of persons are intentionality, consciousness and free agency. We have explored Dennett's treatments of the first two. A system counts as intentional just in case there is a real pattern in its behaviour discernible from the intentional stance, i.e., on the assumption that it has goals, access to information about the world, and makes rational decisions based on these. A system counts as conscious just in case the control system that directs its behaviour implements a 'Joycean machine' – the amplification of different streams of information processing to disproportionate influence on the overall system, in an orderly, linear sequence, controlled by habits of self-stimulation. In the next chapter, I turn to Dennett's account of the third central concept of the manifest image of persons: free agency.

Freedom for Homo sapiens!

Preamble

According to the manifest image, most human beings are *persons*. This means, above all, that we are capable of *freely* choosing our actions and, consequently, that we are *responsible* for much of our behaviour. Our conception of ourselves as free, responsible agents is central to our self-understanding: as I pointed out in chapter 1, many of our most important political, social and economic institutions depend on the assumption that human beings are often responsible for what they do. Yet human freedom seems perplexing: it is hard to see how to reconcile it with *any* causal explanation of human behaviour.

The problem of freedom of the will can be stated with deceptive simplicity. If our behaviour is causally *determined* by factors beyond our control, be it the will of an omniscient and omnipotent being, or the laws governing the atoms of which we are composed, or our genetic endowment, or our early childhood experiences, then it is hard to see how we can do otherwise than we do. To choose freely, in a way that makes you responsible for your choice, is to be able to have chosen otherwise. If your choice is *inevitable*, given the causes that determine it, then, apparently, you cannot choose otherwise. It follows that, despite appearances, you cannot choose freely, in a way that makes you responsible for your choice.

This is the standard argument for *incompatibilism*: the view that causal *determinism* about human behaviour and freedom of the will are incompatible. Anyone who accepts this argument faces a difficult choice: either they must give up determinism and accept that some human behaviour *cannot* be causally explained by the events that precede it, or they must give up freedom of the will and accept that free choice and responsibility are illusions. The first horn of this dilemma is called 'libertarianism'.[1] Libertarians claim that some human behaviour is the result of free choice in virtue of being *undetermined* by preceding events. For this reason, libertarians are often called 'indeterminists'. The second horn of the dilemma is called 'hard determinism'. Hard determinism is the view that no human behaviour is free, that freedom of the will and responsibility are illusions, in virtue of the fact that all human behaviour is causally determined by events that precede it.

Many philosophers, humanists, religious thinkers and other 'guardians' of the manifest image, endorse libertarianism. Hard determinism, on the other hand, is favoured by many scientists. Dennett, as usual, stakes out a middle ground. He rejects the argument for incompatibilism: he thinks that determinism is compatible with freedom of the will. This position is called 'compatibilism' or 'soft determinism'. Compatibilists like Dennett must wage a two-front war: they must argue, against libertarians, that all human behaviour is determined, while at the same time arguing, against hard determinists, that some human behaviour is freely chosen.

This is familiar ground to Dennett: any attempt to reconcile the manifest with the scientific images must wage such a two-front war. We have seen how Dennett defends intentionality and consciousness against eliminativists, while at the same time defending the scientific treatment of these phenomena against dualists. However, Dennett's approach to human freedom is slightly different from his approach to these other two components of the manifest image. Regarding intentionality and consciousness, Dennett acknowledges that reconciliation with the scientific image requires doing some violence to the *ordinary* concepts of these phenomena.[2] However, when it comes to the manifest concept of free will, Dennett is less willing to cede the ground of common sense: he argues that the *ordinary* concept of free will, the only variety of free will 'worth wanting' (ER), is compatible with determinism, and that *incompatibilist* notions of free will do violence to the ordinary concept.

This chapter proceeds as follows. First, I explain Dennett's reasons for claiming that the ordinary concept of free will is compatible with determinism. Next, I examine Dennett's arguments against incompatibilists. Here, I first discuss his responses to libertarians, with special attention to his criticisms of indeterminism and, second, I discuss his interpretation of some recent data from cognitive neuroscience, which some cognitive scientists interpret as incompatible with the efficacy of conscious will. In the third part of the chapter, I explore Dennett's proposals regarding the evolution of human freedom, that is, the evolution of the kind of freedom that is relevant to moral responsibility.

Determinism and true 'evitability'

The claim that if all human behaviour is completely determined by events that precede it then all human behaviour is *inevitable*, is the cornerstone of incompatibilism. If a behaviour is inevitable, then there is nothing we can do to change it. Dennett thinks that this claim relies on a deviant understanding of inevitability. According to Dennett, to say that something is inevitable is to say that it is unavoidable (FE, p. 56), and whether or not some event is avoidable is always relative to an *agent*: (un)avoidable by *whom* (ER, p. 123)? Nothing is inevitable or unavoidable absolutely. To raise the question of inevitability is implicitly to raise this question for a particular agent.

What, for Dennett, is an agent? I discussed this in chapter 2: for Dennett, any system that has interests and, therefore, reasons to act one way rather than another, is an agent of sorts. In other words, any intentional system is, for Dennett, an agent. So the question of whether some event is inevitable or not depends, according to Dennett, on which intentional system is in question. Does it make sense to say that some things are *not* inevitable for, or *avoidable* by, specific intentional systems? Dennett points out that we make such claims all of the time, *even when we know that the behaviour of the agent in question is completely determined by events that precede it.*

Consider two chess-playing computer programs, A and B, pitted against each other in a chess tournament (FE, pp. 77–83). The opening moves of each game are chosen at random, relying on the output of a random number generator, and this generates an indefinite number of games that unfold differently from each other. These chess-playing programs are completely deterministic systems. Every move can be predicted, with perfect precision, based on preceding moves and knowledge of the programs: yet it still makes sense to ask whether some moves are avoidable. Suppose that A beats B ninety per cent of the time, and that this appears to result from B's tendency to move the Queen out too early. It makes sense for B's programmers to ask whether this behaviour is avoidable. Suppose they tweak B to compensate for this, and B wins three games in a row. Here, again, it makes sense to ask whether these wins were flukes, that is, whether A could have avoided defeat, for example, if the randomly chosen initial moves had been slightly different. The fact that, given the initial moves, the game was determined to unfold the way it did is irrelevant to the questions in which the programmers are interested. They want to know something about the *designs* of the programs: are these designs such that defeat is avoidable in slightly different circumstances? Can the designs be tweaked such that future defeats in similar circumstances are avoided?

From this example, we can conclude that there is *at least one* concept of inevitability that is not implied by determinism. That is, since engineers often speak of systems the behaviour of which is completely determined and predictable, as though they can avoid certain outcomes, determinism does not imply inevitability in the engineer's sense. There are deterministic systems for which certain outcomes are, in this sense, avoidable, or to use Dennett's term, *evitable* (FE, p. 56). To claim that the behaviour of such deterministic systems is not, in the engineer's sense, evitable, because it is physically determined, is, according to Dennett, to commit a *category mistake*. One applies a concept that belongs at the level of the *design stance*, in describing a system from the *physical stance* (ER, pp. 139–43; FE, pp. 26, 43, 62, 79).

When an engineer wonders whether certain behaviours of a system they designed are avoidable, they are concerned with the *design* of the system, not with the chain of physical causation that determines the system's behaviour on a particular occasion. If the system does something they do not want it to do, if there is a flaw in its design, then the claim that the behaviour is inevitable, because the system is physically determined to do it in just those circumstances, misses the point of the engineer's concern. They know the system is determined; the question is: can it be designed better, so that, in the future, it avoids the undesired behaviour? This design-level, or engineering notion of avoidability is also relevant in biology. Whether or not the behaviour of organisms is completely determined by preceding events, one cannot understand organisms without employing the concept of avoidability (ER, pp. 126–7; FE, p. 60). Part of the point of a gazelle's legs, for example, is to avoid predators. This follows from Dennett's understanding of biological systems: according to him, they are products of the long, myopic design process made possible by natural selection.[3] As we saw in chapter 2, for this reason, much of their behaviour is best explained from the design stance.

Given that there is one sense of inevitability according to which determinism does not imply it, this raises the question: is this the sense of inevitability that is relevant to the question of human freedom? Or is the incompatibilist sense of inevitability, according to which determinism *does* imply it, the sense that is relevant to the question of human freedom? Dennett argues that the sense of inevitability invoked by engineers when evaluating the designs of deterministic systems is our ordinary sense of inevitability, the sense that is relevant to the question of human freedom. The incompatibilist sense of inevitability is a deviant sense that has no application in everyday life. According to Dennett, incompatibilists make two errors: (1) they misconstrue our ordinary notions of causation and possibility as implying that if an event is causally determined then it is impossible for it not to occur, and (2) they assume that determinism implies that our characters are fixed.

Dennett anchors his discussion of our ordinary notions of causation and possibility in a famous case proposed by the philosopher John Austin as an illustration of incompatibilism (Austin 1961, p. 166; FE, p. 75). Suppose a golfer, mustering all of their skill and the utmost concentration, attempts and fails to hole a putt. Austin asks, was this inevitable? Or, equivalently, was it *impossible* for the golfer to hole the putt? Austin argues that, if determinism is true, then the miss was inevitable; holing the putt on that occasion was impossible. He reasons as follows. If determinism is true, then, given a set of conditions, there is only one possible result. Since prior conditions *determine* subsequent results, whenever two sets of prior conditions are *exactly the same*, the same subsequent results will follow. For this reason, if determinism is true, the golfer, on that occasion, *could* not have holed the putt. Given those *precise* conditions, exactly the same swing, the same grass length on the green, the same surface conditions on the putter, the same wind conditions, etc., it was inevitable that the putt would miss.

Dennett argues that this is not our ordinary understanding of the relation between causation and possibility (FE, pp. 75–7). When we ask whether an event which happened might not have happened, we are not interested in whether it might not have happened in precisely the same circumstances. For one thing, we are never in precisely the same circumstances twice: our sensitivity to new information and our memories makes this impossible (ER, p. 137). Because of this, we are always interested in uncovering *invariant* causal factors at work in past events. This is because we want information that we can use in the future, i.e. *projectible* information (FE, p. 82). The only way to uncover such projectible information about invariant causal factors is to *vary* some of the initial circumstances. For example, in order to determine whether the golfer could have holed the putt, we must alter certain variables to uncover the invariant factors that are causally relevant to successful putts. But this is just the kind of tweaking that engineers do to improve the design of systems like computer programs. And, relative to such tweaking of initial circumstances, the result need not be inevitable: it might be possible to hole the putt, for example, if the circumstances are slightly different.

According to Dennett, the second error in incompatibilist understandings of determinism has to do with their assumption that determinism implies that our characters are fixed (FE, pp. 89–90). Although determinism might imply that our *futures* are fixed, this does not imply that our *characters* are fixed. One can be determined to constantly change one's character. For example, some computers are programmed to learn, thereby constantly changing their responsive dispositions. If human beings are like such systems, then, argues Dennett, the future must *appear* open to human beings. Here is where incompatibilists challenge Dennett. An *apparently* open future, they argue, is not the same as a *truly* open future. According to the incompatibilist, if human beings are deterministic systems, then though our futures may *seem* open to us, they are not *really* open. We have no real options, no real room for self-improvement. An omniscient intelligence, like Laplace's demon,[4] that knew the entire state of the universe at a time before any human being existed, could predict every decision made by every human being that ever came into being.

Dennett replies that the kind of possibility relevant to the question of free will is *subjective* or *epistemic* possibility (ER, pp. 113, 122, 125–6, 147–8; FE, pp. 91, 93). The range of possibilities relevant to an agent's decision-making consists in what is possible *for all the agent knows*, not in what is *truly* possible, and since no possible agent can know exactly what the future holds *for it*, the future must appear subjectively open for every agent.

Any cognitive system has what Dennett calls an 'epistemic horizon' (FE, p. 91): it cannot know every fact about the world it inhabits. This is not just a contingent limitation on memory, sensory capacities and computational powers; it is a *logical* limit on what any possible cognitive system can know about its own states and its own future behaviour (BS, pp. 254–5; ER, p. 112; FE, p. 91). Suppose some cognitive system, like a human being, tries to predict what it will do next by determining its precise, current state. This cannot be done without changing the state the system is in: to learn what state it is in, the system must acquire this information, thereby changing its state. This inevitable change potentially falsifies any prediction based on the information. Or consider the following possibility: another person determines your current state and predicts what you will do. The problem is that the only way *you* could make use of this prediction is by being *told* the prediction, and this inevitably changes your state, potentially falsifying the prediction. If you are told that you are going to be in a traffic accident at 5 p.m. at the corner of Union and Court Streets, then this alters your beliefs in a way that likely falsifies the prediction: you are now *determined*, by your new beliefs, to avoid this intersection at 5 p.m.

In general, any cognitive system, whether a limited physical system like a human being, or an unlimited system like Laplace's demon, cannot take the same attitude towards its own current states and future behaviour as it does towards the current states and future behaviour of other systems. Whether or not we are determined, when it comes to planning our behaviour, we must assume that the future is open. We cannot predict our own behaviour with any precision, on logical grounds. There is always a range of possibilities compatible with any *knowledge* a human being could possibly have about her own states and their future consequences. It is this range of *epistemic* possibilities that is relevant to the question of human freedom. Because we cannot know what our future holds, on logical grounds, we must act as though it is open and, to some extent, up to us. We must act on the assumption that the information we acquire, and the decisions we make on the basis of it can make a difference to which epistemic possibility is actualized. This is the case whether or not our behaviour is determined (ER, p. 113).

The incompatibilist might argue that this is not enough. Even if it is impossible to know what the future holds and one must make decisions from this epistemically limited perspective, in reality, these decisions are inevitable, whether one knows it or not. The future, as a matter of fact, independently of what we know, is closed. Perhaps, but, argues Dennett, this has nothing to do with determinism (ER, pp. 121–2; FE, p. 93). On any view, if it is *true* that something will happen in the future, then there is nothing anyone can do about it. One can do nothing about what *will* happen, whether determinism is true or not. One can only do something about what one *thinks* might happen, given one's inevitably imperfect state of knowledge (ER, pp. 124–6). And since this is the perspective any cognitive system inevitably occupies vis-à-vis its own future behaviour, it must treat its future as open, and its behaviour as, to some extent, under its control. This epistemic sense of possibility is the sense that is relevant to the question of human freedom. Even a deterministic cognitive system cannot help but treat its own future as a range of different possibilities which it has the power to actualize.

The incompatibilist understanding of inevitability and associated notions like possibility and causality do not, and cannot, reflect the ordinary senses of these concepts as they are employed in planning by real cognitive systems, like human beings. Such systems cannot know their futures, and must extract useful information from the past to help determine which of the futures epistemically open to them are actualized. These are precisely the skills that evolution has selected for in human beings and other animals. According to Dennett, we are self-redesigners (DDI, p. 70): we learn from past experience to redesign ourselves in ways that enable us to actualize the futures we want from the set of epistemically possible futures we project. For this reason, the question of whether anything is inevitable for us is a question that only makes sense at the design level: it is the engineer's question. Since we can redesign ourselves to better achieve futures that we want, from the design stance our behaviour is not inevitable.

The sense of inevitability at work in incompatibilist thought experiments like Austin's putt is, according to Dennett, a deviant sense. It involves a category mistake: the misapplication of a design-level concept to the physical level, at which questions of improved design aimed at realizing desired epistemic possibilities make no sense. This is clear when we compare two variants of Austin's case. As described above, the golfer tries their utmost to hole the putt and fails. In such circumstances, it at least *seems* right to say that the miss is inevitable. However, consider a case where the golfer is impaired and careless. Suppose they are hung over and fail to pay attention to their stance or their swing, etc. In such circumstances, it seems right to say that the miss is *not* inevitable: we want to say that, had the golfer been well rested, and concentrated on their stance and swing, the putt would have been holed. Why do our intuitions vary between these two cases? According to the incompatibilist, there is no relevant difference between the two cases. If determinism is true, then missing the putt is inevitable in either case, and if determinism is false, then missing the putt is evitable in either case. Dennett's view that questions of evitability are design-level questions makes much better sense of the cleavage in intuitions here. In the first case, the missed putt seems inevitable because there is no room for self-redesign: the golfer is at their best. In the second case, the missed putt seems evitable because there is a lot of room for self-redesign: the golfer is impaired.

The issue of whether different outcomes are possible in physically identical circumstances is, according to Dennett, an 'idle metaphysical curiosity' (FE, p. 94) of no possible relevance to the question of whether human actions are inevitable. The kind of inevitability that is relevant to the question of whether or not human actions are free concerns our capacity to avoid certain epistemic possibilities based on projectible knowledge we have acquired from past experience. It is clear that much human behaviour is not inevitable in this sense.

Defusing arguments for incompatibilism

Libertarianism

Dennett has identified a variety of free will that is compatible with determinism. Furthermore, he has argued that it corresponds to what we ordinarily mean by 'free will', or at least any variety of free will worth wanting. Are there any other varieties of free will worth wanting? Libertarians argue that there are.

On one view, the kind of free will we really want involves the notion of 'agent causation' (Chisholm 1982). Agent causation is the idea that agents cause events *directly*, not in virtue of being in any particular state. You, not your desire for beer and your belief that there is beer in the fridge, are the ultimate cause of the fridge being opened. Dennett is dismissive of this view (ER, p. 76; FE, p. 100). He finds it mysterious: what explains why you decided to open the fridge, if not your beliefs and desires at the time? The appeal to agent causation, according to Dennett, is an appeal to a supernatural 'unmoved mover', and is incompatible with everything science tells us about the world.

Another variety of libertarianism gets a more sympathetic hearing from Dennett (FE, chapter 4). According to indeterminists like Kane (1996), the kind of free will we really want involves episodes of decision-making that are undetermined by previous states of the mind–brain. For Kane, this does not involve anything 'spooky'. According to quantum physics, at the scale of subatomic particles, natural processes are irreducibly indeterministic: prior states do not *determine* later states; rather, they merely make some later states more *probable* than others. On an influential interpretation of quantum physics, luck or chance are built into the very fabric of the universe. Kane argues that the kind of free will that grounds judgements of moral responsibility can only be explained in terms of the amplification of indeterministic quantum effects to macroscopic scales in the mind–brain, during decision-making. Otherwise, argues Kane, the 'buck cannot stop' with the agent, because any decision can always be blamed on a chain of causes, over which the agent has no control, that determines the decision.

Kane agrees with Dennett that, in many situations, people are held responsible even though they cannot do otherwise. For example, Dennett often appeals to the case of Martin Luther in defence of his view that moral responsibility does *not* require the ability to do otherwise, and is therefore compatible with determinism (ER, p. 133). When asked to recant his alleged heresy, Luther refused, and famously added, 'Here I stand; I can do no other.' As Dennett points out, Luther's claim is not an attempt to duck responsibility. Dennett interprets this case as an example of an action that is free, in the sense of warranting an assignment of moral responsibility, yet, at the same time, determined. In fact, argues Dennett, Luther is responsible *because* his actions are determined *in the right way*, by a process of rational deliberation.

On this view, we are held responsible for such determined actions because they are the result of consciously adopting a policy of preparing for a tough choice, by arranging to *be determined to do the right thing*, when the time comes.

Kane agrees that most actions for which humans are held morally responsible are determined in this way. However, he argues that if *all* episodes of reasoning and decision-making that lead up to such determined behaviours are themselves determined by prior events, then no such assignment of moral responsibility can be warranted. If all of an agent's bouts of reasoning and decision-making are determined, ultimately, by events over which the agent has no control,[5] then they cannot be responsible for any behaviour that results from their reasoning and decision-making. According to Kane, the chain of events leading up to any behaviour for which an agent is responsible must start with some event that is not determined by prior events.

Kane calls such regress-stopping episodes of reasoning 'self-forming actions' (Kane 1996, p. 78). In rare cases, conflicting desires are so well balanced that one faces the problem of Buridan's Ass, the mythical beast that died from indecision, equidistant from food and water (ER, p. 69n; FE, p. 125). In such cases, there are equally compelling reasons to go both ways, so a randomizing factor is very useful: the rational thing to do is to flip a coin. According to Kane, in the mind–brain such coin-flips consist in the amplification of *truly random* quantum-level phenomena to macroscopic effects. The decisions that one arranges to be determined to make, like Luther's refusal to recant, are free and warrant responsibility, *only if* they can be traced to such undetermined, self-forming actions.

Dennett's objection to Kane's proposal is simple. How can tracing the pedigree of one's behaviour to a self-forming action be so important, if there is absolutely no way to tell whether or not some self-forming action is *truly* random, or merely pseudo-random? It is possible for completely deterministic systems to mimic random processes. The operation of computers relies on the generation of random numbers by pseudo-random number generators. These are programs that are completely deterministic: they do not draw on information from any truly random phenomena. However, for all practical purposes, the numbers they generate are random, that is, *patternless*. This is because they draw on information[6] that, though determined, has absolutely no relevance to the functions for which computers use the numbers. If the brain used such a pseudo-random process to prod itself out of motivational ruts, could we tell the difference between such pseudo-self-forming actions and Kane's genuinely undetermined self-forming actions?

Clearly, persons could not tell which of their own decisions were genuinely random as opposed to pseudo-random self-forming actions. One cannot tell whether some event in one's mind is the result of the amplification of some quantum phenomenon through introspection. And it is extremely unlikely that neuroimaging technology capable of tracing some brain state to a sub-atomic quantum event will ever be available. But if the warrant of assignments of moral responsibility *depends* on whether some action can be traced to a genuinely random rather than a pseudo-random self-forming action, then, on Kane's theory, we have never known assignments of moral responsibility to be warranted, and we will never know them to be warranted, unless extremely unlikely neuroimaging technology becomes available. This, according to Dennett, reduces Kane's proposal to absurdity (FE, pp. 127, 131).[7]

Dennett offers the following diagnosis of Kane's motivations. He is driven by *essentialistic* assumptions that have no place in a Darwinian world (FE, pp. 126–7). Essentialism is the view that entities, like mammals, or events, like free decisions warranting assignments of responsibility, have *essences*: properties that an entity or an event *must* have in order to count as an entity or event of some type. To use Dennett's example, one might claim that mammals have the following essential property: every mammal must have mammal parents (ER, pp. 84–5). If this were true, then there would be no mammals, for, the theory of evolution implies that there was a time when there were no mammals, and if there were no mammals at one time, then nothing could ever have mammals as parents, so there would still be no mammals. The dilemma is resolved once we appreciate that most categories have vague boundaries. There is no 'Prime Mammal' (FE, pp. 126–7);

non-mammals gradually grade into mammals through all sorts of intermediate, quasi-mammal forms. This is one of the revolutionary ideas implied by Darwin's theory of evolution. Similarly, argues Dennett, there are no regress-stopping self-forming actions that are founts of all freedom and responsibility in a person's life. Events for which we are not responsible gradually grade into events for which we are responsible, through all sorts of intermediate, quasi-responsible forms, through childhood and adolescence (FE, pp. 135–6).

Hard determinism

Dennett's moves on one incompatibilist front are matched by moves on the other incompatibilist front: according to Dennett, just as libertarians fail to make the case for a variety of free will at odds with determinism, hard determinists fail to make the case that free will is an illusion. The main source of contemporary scepticism regarding the efficacy of conscious will is a series of counterintuitive results relating subjects' brain activity to their reports of conscious decision-making. There is a very reliable spike in brain activity, known as a readiness potential, that precedes any voluntary motion. The cognitive neuroscientist Benjamin Libet devised an experiment for plotting a subject's conscious decision to initiate a motion against the readiness potential that invariably precedes the motion in the brain (Libet 1999, p. 49; FE, pp. 227–9). He asked subjects to decide, spontaneously, to flick their wrists, while watching a clock with a rotating 'dot' that indicated the time, and to note the position of the dot when they make the conscious decision. Libet found that the time that subjects report they make their decision lags behind the onset of the readiness potential, which indicates the flick is already in the works, by up to half a second – a very long time in neural terms. Libet draws the following implication from this research: conscious will cannot initiate actions. Actions are initiated by unconscious processes in the brain, long before we are aware of them and, at best, conscious will has about a tenth of a second to modulate the action the brain has already begun (FE, pp. 229–31).

Although this does not amount to the claim that conscious will is *entirely* illusory, it does approach a hard determinist position. Conscious will is, at the very least, far less involved in the initiation of action than we take it to be.

Dennett must find other interpretations of this evidence. His project of *reconciling* the scientific with the manifest images depends on explaining how conscious will could still be efficacious in the light of such evidence. The seeds of a response are already contained in Dennett's theory of the conscious self. To interpret Libet's evidence as showing that the efficacy of conscious will is illusory is, according to Dennett, to be in the grip of the Cartesian Theatre model of the conscious mind (FE, p. 244). In other words, it is to misapply the manifest image boundary between an agent and her environment to processes *within* the brain. In chapter 3, I discussed Dennett's claim that the Cartesian Theatre is an artefact of this kind of category mistake: the distinction between observed and unobserved events, which makes perfect sense when applied to whole persons at ordinary timescales, is mistakenly applied to the brief time scales of processes going on within brains. Libet's conclusions about the inefficacy of conscious will make a similar mistake. As Dennett points out repeatedly throughout *Freedom Evolves* (2003), if you make the self really small, you can externalize almost everything (FE, p. 122).[8] Libet's conclusions are based on the assumption that the self must be 'punctate' (FE, p. 122n), i.e., unextended in space and time. Because the evidence shows that there is no work for such punctate selves to do in the brain, he concludes that the efficacy of conscious will is an illusion. But, argues Dennett, all this research shows is that the conscious self is spread out in time and space: that conscious decisions take time (FE, pp. 242, 246).

Dennett questions the assumption, of both libertarians and hard determinists, that for conscious will to be real and efficacious, it must exist in some small, well defined spatiotemporal domain within the brain. The conscious self is much 'larger' than the neural activity immediately preceding some action. As we saw in chapter 4, the self encompasses all the activity that can be woven into a coherent self-defining narrative. There is no reason why something that happens very quickly and unconsciously, immediately before an action, should fail to count as a decision *you* have made, a decision for which *you* are responsible. Professional tennis players return serves that travel 75 feet at over 100 miles per hour. This gives them less than half a second to respond. Are such responses consciously willed (FE, p. 238)? On Libet's view, they cannot be, because half a second takes up all the time of the readiness potential. But surely professional tennis players are responsible for such responses and, in some sense, consciously will them. The puzzle is resolved when we appreciate that the will is spread out in time. Just as Luther did a lot of work to turn himself into the kind of person that is determined to do the right thing when challenged, professional tennis players turn themselves into 'situation-action machines' (FE, p. 238), determined to respond skilfully and extremely quickly in tennis matches. In both cases, the agent is responsible not because there is a punctate self calling the shots in the millisecond before the action, but because the action is determined by a brain mechanism that the agent, earlier, during practice and training, *designed* to respond that way. We are responsible for our behaviour not because we are consciously involved in every decision, but because we consciously set our brains up such that they are determined to respond, automatically, the way we want them to respond, in different situations.

Dennett's complaints have a distinctively Rylean flavour. Kane's search for concrete, datable, genuinely random self-forming actions is as misguided as Libet's search for the precise time and place of conscious decision in the brain. The search for conscious will at such microscopic, neural scales is a category mistake. There is no concrete, datable, conscious will in the brain. The categories 'conscious will' and 'conscious self' apply not to brief activity in *parts* of the brain at specific times, but to spatio-temporally extended patterns of activity by whole persons. All it takes to have an efficacious will that issues in behaviour, for which a conscious self is responsible, is to be a sophisticated, self-redesigning system: a system controlled by a Joycean machine that enables it to respond flexibly to information about the past, by changing itself in ways that enable it to better pursue its goals in the future.

And this is precisely the kind of system that human beings are, thanks to a unique and wonderful evolutionary history.

The evolution of morally significant free will

The kind of compatibilist freedom discernible from the design stance, the freedom to learn from one's mistakes to avoid undesired epistemic possibilities in the future, is an important variety of free will often overlooked in philosophical discussions of the free will problem. However, it cannot be sufficient for *morally* significant free will. This is because any animal capable of envisioning alternate future courses of behaviour, and selecting one on the basis of past experience,[9] is free in this sense. However, we do not treat non-human animals as morally responsible for their behaviour. Warrants are not issued for the arrest of cheetahs involved in gazelle murders. Since human freedom must explain moral responsibility, it must consist in something more than merely the freedom to redesign oneself, in response to past mistakes, in order to avoid undesired epistemic possibilities in the future.

On the traditional, philosophical understanding of the relationship between moral responsibility and freedom, judgements of moral responsibility depend on prior judgements of freedom. That is, a person is held responsible for actions that we know, on independent grounds, the person chose to perform freely. According to the traditional view, if a person cannot act otherwise than they act, then they are not morally responsible for the action. This understanding of the relationship between moral responsibility and freedom is problematic for the determinist. Strictly speaking, for any action that any deterministic agent performs, the agent cannot do otherwise. On the traditional philosophical understanding of the relationship between moral responsibility and human freedom, if human beings are deterministic agents, then they are never truly morally responsible, because they can never do otherwise than they do. This raises what Dennett calls 'the Spectre of Creeping Exculpation' (FE, p. 21): it seems that, the more we learn about the causes of human behaviour, the more we must excuse moral transgressions. But Dennett argues that the traditional philosophical understanding of the relationship between moral responsibility and human freedom is incorrect.

Following Stephen White (1991), Dennett proposes that we *invert* the traditional priority of judgements of freedom to judgements of moral responsibility (FE, p. 297). Rather than grounding judgements of moral responsibility in prior judgements of freedom, or ability to do otherwise, Dennett urges that we judge that people are able to do otherwise in situations in which there are good, independent reasons to hold them responsible. Whether or not an agent can *really* do otherwise is irrelevant. If there is good independent reason to hold an agent morally responsible for some action, then the agent must be treated as if they can do otherwise. White argues that the ideal system of punishment is one in which the person punished *sees* the punishment as justified. In effect, as Dennett puts it, the person takes a 'Thanks, I needed that' attitude towards the punishment (FE, pp. 297, 301). Or, in other words, whether or not the person could have done otherwise, they *take* responsibility for their actions, thereby gaining control over them in the future. According to Dennett, this practice of taking responsibility, whether or not one could have done otherwise, is central to the variety of free will that is relevant to moral responsibility (ER, p. 165; FE, p. 292). In Dennett's terms, we make ourselves '*large*' (FE, p. 302) by accepting responsibility for actions that we may not have fully controlled, thereby increasing our freedom, i.e., our control of those types of actions in the future.

So, the question of whether or not we are free in the sense that moral responsibility requires becomes, for Dennett, the question of whether the practice of taking responsibility, and thereby making ourselves larger, is a practice in which we want to engage. And the answer to *this* question is, according to Dennett, obvious. Of course we want to take responsibility. To be treated as *not* responsible, as impaired in one's capacity for rational self-control, is to lose many of the most prized opportunities available to human beings. As Dennett puts it, 'Blame is the price we pay for credit, and we pay it gladly under most circumstances. We pay dearly, accepting punishment and public humiliation for a chance to get back in the game after we have been caught out in some transgression' (FE, p. 292). So, for Dennett, the kind of freedom that comes with moral responsibility arises from our desire to participate in the practice of *taking* responsibility for our inevitable lapses, whether or not any particular lapse is determined to happen. In order to understand how this kind of freedom evolved from the mere freedom to self-redesign that we share with non-human animals, we must understand why the practice of taking responsibility was selected for in human evolution.

As we saw in chapter 4, according to Dennett, the capacity for sophisticated cultural learning is the central innovation that drove human evolution. Unlike other organisms, we depend on acquiring skills, passed down in traditions, through cultural learning. But culture depends, essentially, on cooperation. Novices can only be taught if there are teachers willing to share information. Honestly sharing information is an essentially cooperative act: an honest communicator ignores their narrow self-interest and divulges information, despite the fact that keeping it secret may give them a competitive advantage over potential competitors. Such cooperation calls for special evolutionary explanations. This is because refusing to cooperate, or 'defecting' in the jargon of game theory, is what the biologist John Maynard-Smith calls an 'evolutionarily stable strategy' (FE, p. 149). In many circumstances, when defectors interact with cooperators, defectors win. This is a consequence of the structure of many forms of interaction among organisms. Maynard-Smith shows that interactions among organisms often have the structure of what economists call a prisoner's dilemma.

In prisoner's dilemmas, the best outcome of an interaction for an individual occurs when the other party cooperates while the individual defects. In the classic example from which the dilemma gets its name, two arrested co-conspirators are offered deals by the prosecutor. If they cooperate *with each other*, by refusing to deal with the prosecutor, the prosecutor can only hold them for a year because there is not enough evidence. If one caves, ratting out or defecting against the other prisoner, who cooperates by staying quiet, the rat is freed and the other prisoner is imprisoned for ten years. If they both cave, ratting out or defecting against each other, then they both get five years. Although, in the aggregate, it is obvious that the first option is the best – each only gets one year in prison – from the perspective of each prisoner, defecting appears the best. If the other cooperates, this gives the defector immediate freedom, as opposed to one year imprisonment if they cooperate. If the other defects, this gives the defector five years, as opposed to ten years if they cooperate. Given this structure, defection is always rational. If this is the structure of many forms of interaction among organisms, then how does cooperation ever evolve?

Primitive forms of cooperation, such as the symbiosis that led to the evolution of eukaryotic cells and the behaviour of social insects, show that prisoner's dilemmas are not inevitable (FE, pp. 145, 150, 198). Dennett argues that the practice of taking responsibility evolved among human beings as the result of a distinctively hominid form of cooperation, a kind of cooperation that made culture possible. The first stage, which inaugurated cultural evolution, involved the development of a practice of enforcing conformity to cooperative norms through punishment. As Boyd and Richerson (1992) show, if punishment is cheap, then group conformity can emerge in a population. So, according to Dennett, our hominid precursors took a first step towards culture when they evolved various mechanisms for maintaining group conformity, including a preference for conformity and a disposition to punish nonconformists (FE, pp. 201–2).

Such circumstances would likely lead to an evolutionary 'arms race'. Individuals capable of faking conformity to some norm, e.g., sexual fidelity, until defection paid off, e.g., when mates were not around, would gain certain advantages. But this would lead to selection for individuals capable of detecting fakers. A spiral of increasing abilities to fake and to detect fakers would ensue. In such circumstances, individuals who could both resist the temptation to defect and gain a reputation for honouring cooperative norms would have a tremendous advantage (FE, p. 204). This, according to Dennett, led to the next stage in the evolution of morally relevant human freedom. Drawing on some proposals by Frank (1988), Dennett argues that, in response to such circumstances, our ancestors evolved hard-to-fake, *emotional* signals of commitment to future courses of behaviour. The best way to gain a reputation for cooperation and commitment to norms, that is, a reputation for being good, is to actually be good (FE, pp. 204–5). And the way to be good is to turn oneself into the kind of individual that cannot help but do good: to design oneself to *reliably* ignore temptations and do the right thing when the occasion arises. Furthermore, the best way to do this is to develop emotional commitments to certain courses of behaviour that trump the hyperrational, micro-managed pursuit of self-interest that leads to prisoner's dilemmas (FE, p. 214).

We resist temptation, according to Dennett, by engaging in a kind of intra-personal, intertemporal bargaining (FE, pp. 210–11).[10] Because we know that, in the heat of the moment, when faced with temptation, it is difficult not to yield,[11] we use this information when bargaining with our future, inevitably tempted selves. And, in this bargaining, we try to make offers that our future selves cannot refuse: emotion-laden 'sticks' and 'carrots' capable of counteracting future temptations of the moment. For example, individuals capable of intense shame or guilt can use these emotions as bargaining chips: when moments of temptation arise, the prospect of inevitable future shame or guilt trumps temptation. In addition, emotion-based, hard-to-fake signals of social commitment, of the kind that Frank proposes as means of gaining a good reputation, develop as a by-product of such emotional commitment to courses of action in our personal lives (FE, pp. 213–14). So, the capacity to use emotions to make ourselves into the kinds of individuals for whom most temptations do not arise was likely to evolve in the circumstances of our precursors. This is because, in such circumstances, individuals capable of resisting temptation and gaining a reputation for commitment to cooperative endeavours would be selected for (FE, pp. 214–15).

According to Dennett, such capacities include components of morally significant free will. For example, intra-personal, intertemporal bargaining involves self-prediction of a kind that makes future behaviour indeterminate to the agent (FE, pp. 211–12). Consider an alcoholic bargaining with their future, tempted self.[12] They predict that they are likely to succumb to temptation in certain circumstances, but this prediction leads them to propose new incentives to their future self aimed at avoiding such circumstances, thereby falsifying that prediction. This is precisely the kind of dynamic, discussed above, that makes any cognitive system's future behaviour unpredictable to itself: any prediction alters the system's state, thereby potentially falsifying itself. Such dynamics make the agent's future behaviour unpredictable, whether or not it is physically determined (FE, p. 211). Furthermore, once the capacity to make oneself emotionally committed evolved, our precursors were capable of the kind of Lutherian self-design that Dennett identifies as the basis of moral responsibility. Just as Martin Luther trained himself to be the kind of individual who can do no other, our immediate precursors evolved capacities for emotional commitment that insured resistance to future temptation. Contrary to the traditional understanding of moral responsibility, determinism, argues Dennett, actually explains our status as moral agents: a moral agent can make themselves such that they are *determined* to do the right thing (FE, pp. 216–17).

In order to reach this stage, our precursors had to develop sophisticated capacities for self-monitoring and self-control. Such capacities require abilities to predict likely future behaviour, and to set up ways of preventing some behaviours and encouraging others. But sophisticated self-prediction and self-control appear next to impossible for creatures with neural control systems as complex as ours. How can we gain any purchase on what our complicated brains are likely to do? According to Dennett, the key innovation that made sophisticated self-prediction and self-control possible for our precursors was the evolution of sophisticated communication (FE, pp. 248–9).

Sophisticated language gives rise to a practice of giving and asking for reasons, and this practice both requires that we keep track of our motivations and simplifies this task by providing ready-made categories for classifying motivational states. Dennett sees this as the source of 'non-obliviousness' (FE, p. 250): the kind of sophisticated self-knowledge and self-control on which the practice of taking responsibility depends. Children are initiated into this practice with constant queries about their reasons for doing things, long before the evidence warrants assumptions of self-knowledge and rationality (FE, pp. 251, 273, 277). The practice of taking responsibility results from this. In order to become effective communicators, that is, effective reason askers and givers, we must be taught, from the start, to take responsibility for events that, initially, we cannot control. We must learn to make ourselves 'larger' than we are. By being given responsibility, we learn to take responsibility. On Dennett's view, the distinctively human variety of free will, on which moral responsibility is based, is a function of this distinctively human form of enculturation: 'Our autonomy does not depend on anything like the miraculous suspension of causation but rather on the integrity of the processes of education and mutual sharing of knowledge' (FE, p. 287).

Last words on freedom and the way forward

The question of human freedom, as philosophers have traditionally understood it, is, for Dennett, 'an idle metaphysical curiosity' (FE, p. 94). It is based on deviant, incompatibilist understandings of inevitability, possibility and causality. For Dennett, any cognitive system that is capable of sophisticated self-redesign is free, whether or not it is determined. Freedom, for Dennett, is a matter of *control* over *future* behaviour, and control is a matter of *knowledge*. The more we know about the causes that determine our behaviour, the more control we have over them in the future and the freer we are. To Dennett, there is no question that human beings have become freer in the past century or so, largely as a consequence of greater knowledge of and control over nature. That we have become freer in this sense is obvious, and does not depend on answering the metaphysical question of whether or not our behaviour is ultimately determined (FE, p. 296). To Dennett, the greatest threats to human freedom are not metaphysical. Freedom depends on knowledge and on playing the game of taking responsibility, and the greatest threats to these sources of freedom are political (FE, pp. 292, 295, 305).

This completes my overview of Dennett's proposed solutions to the three components of the reconciliation problem. In chapter 1, I described Dennett's project as an attempt to show how it can be the case both (1) that human beings are conscious, thinking, free, responsible agents, and (2) that human beings are purely natural products of evolution, composed of simple biochemical components, arranged in complex, self-maintaining configurations. Chapters 2 through 5 have provided an overview of Dennett's proposals. Products of evolution are inevitably intentional systems and, so, according to Dennett, inevitably believers. Human beings are products of a unique evolutionary history in which cooperation, culture and sophisticated communication played important roles. Human consciousness is the result of our being designed, by evolution, to communicate using a sophisticated language. This led to the installation of the Joycean machine on the parallel hardware of the brain. This virtual machine gives rise to the conscious self: a centre of narrative gravity that unifies the stream of consciousness. The Joycean machine has given Homo sapiens powers unparalleled in the natural world: we are capable of sophisticated and flexible self-redesign. Our freedom consists in this capacity: it gives us the power to make ourselves larger by *taking* responsibility, and thereby expand our knowledge and control.

Dennett's vision is highly original and immense in scope. However it raises almost as many questions as it answers. The next chapter is devoted to addressing two of the most controversial assumptions of Dennett's proposals. First, I discuss Dennett's invocations of Darwin's theory of natural selection. This theory is central to Dennett's way of reconciling the scientific with the manifest images: he repeatedly constructs evolutionary narratives aimed at showing how simple systems, to which manifest concepts, like intentionality, consciousness and free will, do not apply, can gradually evolve into complex systems to which such concepts apply. Darwinian accounts of evolution are, however, notoriously controversial and Dennett himself has deemed it necessary to defend his Darwinism against diverse critics (DDI). Second, I discuss Dennett's notion of a real pattern. Dennett follows his teacher Gilbert Ryle in arguing that the problem of reconciling the scientific with the manifest images is largely overstated as a result of the misapplication of manifest concepts to inappropriate domains.

Manifest concepts like the self, consciousness, will and intention-ality apply to overall patterns of behaviour in which whole organ-isms and persons participate, not to microscopic events taking place at brief time scales within the brain. But this claim raises a question concerning the *reality* of these higher-level patterns. Surely the *actual* causal transactions that *really* explain behaviour involve neural and physical events taking place at microscopic scales. Tracking higher-level patterns using manifest concepts might be useful, but in what sense are such higher-level patterns *real*?

Darwin and the game of life

Chapter Six

Preamble

Darwinism is the view that most significant biological phenomena, including the human mind and its cultural products, are products of (some variant of) natural selection. Natural selection is one of the mechanisms proposed by Darwin as an explanation of how biological structures evolve. Living beings must acquire resources to survive and reproduce. These resources are limited, and this inevitably gives rise to competition. Variation is also inevitable among organisms: variation between species is obvious, but variation within species is just as prevalent though more subtle. Since organisms inevitably differ from each other, there will be some that are better at securing resources necessary for survival and reproduction than others. Given that limited resources lead to inevitable competition, organisms better equipped to acquire them will survive longer and reproduce more than others. Since parents pass on their traits, coded in genes, to their offspring, over the long run, populations of organisms will come to be dominated by organisms that are *good* at securing resources necessary for survival and reproduction. This underwrites *adaptationism* – the most controversial component of Darwinism.

According to adaptationism, the prevalence of certain traits in populations of organisms can be explained by showing that they are *adaptive*, i.e., by showing that they play an important role in securing resources necessary for survival and reproduction. This is just a first step. Such *apparent design* must then be explained in terms of the mechanism of natural selection: the adaptationist must explain how the differential reproduction of certain genes, in the environmental circumstances that likely characterized ancestral populations, yielded the distributions of adaptive traits in current populations.

Dennett is one of today's foremost defenders of Darwinian adaptationism. As we have seen, Darwinism plays an important role in Dennett's proposed solution to the reconciliation problem. He explains how thought, consciousness and freedom of the will are possible for physical systems, by showing how simple systems that do not have these might give rise, in evolution, to complex systems that do have them. According to Dennett, we are capable of thought because, at some point in our evolutionary history, our ancestors' superior ability to think gave them advantages over competitors in acquiring resources necessary for survival and reproduction. We are conscious because our ancestors' superior ability to acquire culturally transmitted habits of self-stimulation that control the flow of information in the brain gave them comparable advantages over competitors. Our wills are free, in the morally relevant sense, because our ancestors' superior capacities to take responsibility and commit to courses of action gave them comparable advantages over competitors.

Darwinism plays other fundamental roles in Dennett's thinking. As we saw in chapter 5, in the discussion of Dennett's critique of Kane's indeterminism, it underwrites his fundamental metaphysical viewpoint: anti-essentialism. It even informs his philosophical methodology: Dennett's strategy of retooling traditional manifest concepts for easier integration with the scientific worldview is analogous to Mother Nature's opportunistic redeployment of old resources to new uses in evolution, a phenomenon Dennett calls 'bait and switch' (DDI, p. 214).[1] It is not an exaggeration to say that Dennett's proposals constitute one of the most ambitious applications of Darwinian principles to philosophical problems of the last century. For Dennett, *all* appearance of intelligence and design in nature – from the simplest viruses to the most subtle scientific theories – can and must be explained in terms of Darwinian principles. If one were asked to encapsulate Dennett's proposal regarding the place of mind and meaning in nature in one word, 'Darwinism' would probably be the best candidate.

Dennett's unabashed and exuberant embrace of Darwinian adaptationism defies today's pervasive scepticism of it. Religion-inspired resistance to Darwinism is well known; however, it is also denigrated among secular academics and even among influential biologists. Dennett devotes his longest work, *Darwin's Dangerous Idea* (1995), to debunking the reasons that have been offered for such scepticism. Below, I first locate Dennett's embrace of Darwinism in the context of his overall project. Early in his career, discussion of Artificial Intelligence (AI) was his favoured tool for explaining how the mind could be a physical system. However, over the course of his career, discussion of Darwinian biology has taken over this role, particularly in the wake of the publication of *The Intentional Stance* in 1987. A large portion of *Darwin's Dangerous Idea* is devoted to exploring the strong affinities between AI and Darwinian biology. Dennett argues that Darwinian biology, like AI, is fundamentally an attempt to explain intelligence in terms of unintelligent, algorithmic processes. In the next two sections, I briefly survey many reasons that have been proposed against Darwinism and Dennett's responses. Finally, I focus on one central difficulty with Dennett's understanding of adaptation and intentionality as real patterns discernible from the intentional stance. The worry is that design and mind are merely useful ways of thinking about certain systems, as opposed to real features of the natural world. Dennett's response centres on a computer simulation known as the 'game of life', from which he draws important lessons about what it is for a pattern to be real.

Naturally selected robots

As I pointed out in chapters 1 and 2, one of Dennett's fundamental disagreements with mainstream philosophy of mind concerns the distinction between original/intrinsic intentionality and derived intentionality. Words, pictures and values stored in a computer's memory all have a kind of intentionality: they *stand for* or are *about* things. The word 'cat' stands for cats, and a value stored in a computer's memory might stand for a student's grade on a term paper. But these are clear examples of *derived* intentionality. Artefacts like words, pictures and computer memories are assigned their meanings by human beings: writers, painters and programmers, respectively. For example, a value in my spreadsheet file might stand for a student's grade in virtue of the fact that I intended this and, for this reason, assigned this meaning to this value. The value derives its intentionality from my intention. But my intention has intentionality too: it represents the world the way I intend it to be, i.e., such that the value, in the spreadsheet file, stands for the grade. We can therefore ask the same question of my intention: where does my intention get its intentionality? Dennett argues that many contemporary philosophers are committed to the view that human intentions, and other mental states, do not derive their intentionality from anything. The intentionality of human thoughts is *original* intentionality and, because it derives from nothing outside of us, it is *intrinsic* intentionality (IS, p. 288). This distinction underwrites much philosophical scepticism about the possibility of AI. Since artefacts only have derived intentionality, robots or computers will never be genuine thinkers, in the sense that human beings are.

Dennett defends the possibility of thinking artefacts, like robots, by attempting to dismantle the alleged distinction between original/intrinsic and derived intentionality. According to Dennett, the intentionality of human thought is no less derived than the intentionality of artefacts. His explanation of how the intentionality of human thought can be derived is the crucible in which the alliance between AI and Darwinism, which plays such an important role in his later thought, is forged. Drawing heavily on Richard Dawkins' gene-centred interpretation of Darwin (Dawkins 1976), Dennett argues that human beings are nothing more than evolved robots, and that the intentionality of our mental states derives from our 'designer', namely, the process of natural selection (IS, pp. 295–8; DDI, pp. 422–6). On Dawkins' version of Darwinism, organisms are nothing but survival machines, designed through natural selection, as mechanisms that excel at one job: reproducing the genes that code for their construction.

From this proposal, Dennett draws the following philosophical lessons concerning the alleged distinction between original/intrinsic and derived intentionality. Since we are 'natural robots' 'designed' by natural selection to reproduce genes in certain specific environments, the intentionality of our thoughts does not originate within us; it is derived from our 'designer', natural selection. For this reason, the intentionality of human thought is no more original or intrinsic than the intentionality of artefacts like robots. As a consequence, there is no principled, philosophical barrier to artificial intelligence. Robots will never have original/intrinsic intentionality but neither do we. If humans are genuinely intelligent despite the derived intentionality of our thoughts, then robots and other artefacts can be genuinely intelligent as well. Here we see a dramatic illustration of Dennett's general approach to the reconciliation problem. At the same time as he *deflates* an apparently miraculous human capacity, i.e., original/intrinsic intentionality, he *inflates* our image of a purely mechanical, scientifically tractable phenomenon: natural selection can 'design' machines as elaborate and complex as us.

Once forged, Dennett's integration of AI with Darwinism yields impressive synergies. Dennett points out that the 'strange inversion of reasoning' (DDI, p. 65), whereby Darwin explains design in nature in terms of the mindless process of natural selection, is central to the project of AI as well. Both Darwinism and AI try to explain apparent intelligence in terms of unintelligent, mechanical, *algorithmic* processes.

As we saw in chapter 2, the competence of an artefact can be specified at the intentional level. For example, when we describe a computer that can play chess, we assume that it *knows* the rules of chess, can *perceive* board positions, *desires* to checkmate its opponent and *understands* how to accomplish this goal. But, as we also saw in chapter 2, an intentional description, for Dennett, is only the beginning of the explanatory project: any description at the intentional level takes out loans of intelligence which must be repaid by *distributing* the intelligence across the combined activity of unintelligent, computational components. In AI and cognitive science, these loans are repaid by specifying algorithms, simple procedures broken down into steps that unintelligent, physical mechanisms can accomplish. For example, all of the apparently intelligent capacities of a standard desktop computer are, ultimately, the result of extremely rapid flipping of switches between 'on' and 'off' positions, representing the ones and zeros of binary code.

Dennett points out that Darwinian explanation in biology proceeds in exactly the same way. A phenomenon that apparently requires intelligence, namely, good design, is explained in terms of algorithms – simple procedures broken down into steps that unintelligent, physical mechanisms can accomplish. For example, the adaptationist description of the mammalian eye, as exquisitely designed for the purpose of transducing light into neural signals, constitutes, according to Dennett, an intentional level description that incurs loans of intelligence, which must be repaid. In Darwinian explanations, such loans of intelligence are repaid by *distributing* the design work across millions of generations of natural selection, over the course of which innovations that help genes reproduce gradually accumulate. Just as there is no intelligent homunculus organizing the activity in AI systems, there is no intelligent designer whose purpose is to construct the mammalian eye, or any other exquisitely designed biological structure. In both cases, apparent intelligence and design emerge from myopic mechanisms implementing algorithms.

In the case of evolution, the algorithm is natural selection, which amounts, basically, to the following rule: keep those genes that yield phenotypic effects that allow the genes to reproduce with greatest frequency, compared to competitors. No intelligence is required to follow this algorithm because it is followed automatically. As stated, the algorithm sounds almost vacuous: structures better at reproducing will come to dominate a population of reproducing structures. As Dennett points out, at this level, the natural selection algorithm resembles the algorithm governing the following coin-tossing tournament (DDI, p. 53). Pair off the contestants and have them call a coin-toss. The winners of each pair are paired off again, in a series of rounds, until only one is left. This algorithm is guaranteed to yield a person that has won numerous coin-tosses in a row. Similarly, natural selection is guaranteed to yield organisms constructed from genes that have won the game of reproducing for many generations in a row, but winning the game of reproducing involves more than luck, unlike winning the coin-tossing tournament. Because both variation in ability to reproduce and scarcity of resources required for reproduction prevail in nature, natural selection is guaranteed to yield genes that code for organisms that are *good* at reproducing. This fact rescues natural selection from vacuity and explains why it can yield organisms that are well-designed. As Dennett puts it, Darwinian algorithms, like natural selection, resemble processes of elimination not in tournaments of luck, like the coin-tossing tournament but, rather, in tournaments of *skill*, where winners are more than just lucky; they are good at something (DDI, p. 55).

Even granting this, many find it unbelievable that a myopic, algorithm-following process like natural selection could yield the dramatic feats of intelligence and design that characterize the living world. According to Darwinists like Dennett, this simple algorithm, together with more complex variants of it, are responsible not just for intricate biological structures like mammalian eyes and brains, but also for all products of evolved brains, including all feats of human intelligence and design.

An important implication of Dennett's Darwinism is that the distinction between the natural and the artificial breaks down. This, according to Dennett, follows from Dawkins' version of Darwinism. We are (composed of) natural robots 'designed' by natural selection, so the things we design – artefacts and other cultural products – are ultimately products of natural selection as well. As we saw in chapter 4, culture, transmitted in memes, is part of Homo sapiens' 'extended phenotype'. Because of this, Dawkins' version of Darwinism enables us to locate both natural and artificial structures in one enormous design space that defines the entire set of possible designs (DDI, pp. 135–44). Natural selection and related algorithms are seen as mechanical procedures for exploring this space, for 'finding' actual designs in the vast space of possible designs. Over the eons, these procedures have discovered amoebas, zebras, Ford Model Ts, the Theory of Relativity and countless other denizens of design space. Much vaster numbers remain undiscovered and, of these, unimaginably vast numbers will forever remain undiscovered (DDI, pp. 135–44).

Critics of Darwinism balk at such ambitious extensions of the theory of evolution by natural selection. How can such an unintelligent process be responsible for the greatest feats of design known to us? Dennett agrees that it is often hard to see how algorithmic variants on natural selection can account for some of the more intricate denizens of design space. However, he details numerous elaborations of the basic Darwinian algorithm that dramatically enhance its power. As he notes, often such elaborations are proposed as alternatives to natural selection, necessary to account for some particularly dramatic example of intricate design. But, invariably, they are shown to be entirely consistent with Darwin's basic idea (DDI, pp. 75–6). According to Dennett, this is no accident. Darwin's idea is more than a theory; it is a basic methodological principle that is compulsory for any mystery-free explanation of apparently intelligent design.

As we saw in previous chapters, Dennett has stressed, throughout his career, that explaining intelligent behaviour or design in terms of equally or more intelligent capacities is not explaining them at all. The theory of natural selection is an incredibly powerful alternative to such non-explanations. This is Darwin's central insight. It shows how apparently intelligent design can emerge from a process that is entirely unintelligent. If the simplest variety of natural selection cannot explain some example of apparently intelligent design, then we must search for some more complicated variant of it, which preserves the basic idea that an unintelligent selection mechanism can yield apparently intelligent design.

The yearning for some alternative is, according to Dennett, like the yearning for a skyhook: some miraculously intelligent process, ungrounded in physically realistic mechanisms, capable of lifting simple systems to ever greater heights in design space (DDI, p. 76). This yearning for skyhooks is precisely analogous to the positing of intelligent homunculi that Dennett urges cognitive scientists to avoid.[2] Physically inexplicable intelligence is treated as an unexplained explainer. Instead of skyhooks, Dennett argues that challenging cases of apparently intelligent design call for ever more ingenious 'cranes': variants on natural selection, capable of lifting simple systems through design space, that are *grounded* in physically explicable, unintelligent, mechanical selection processes (DDI, p. 75). The use of 'cranes' in evolutionary biology is precisely analogous to AI's decomposition of intelligent capacities into simpler subcapacities, implemented by progressively less intelligent components, until a level is reached at which entirely unintelligent physical mechanisms can do all the work. A large part of *Darwin's Dangerous Idea* (1995) is devoted to exploring the different sorts of 'cranes' that have been proposed in response to some of the greatest challenges to Darwinism, including the emergence of life from inorganic precursors, the emergence of minds capable of flexible self-redesign and the emergence of culture. I survey some of these elaborations of natural selection below.

In chapter 2, we discussed Dennett's three-stance approach to explaining complex systems. Dennett's assimilation of AI with Darwinism appears to conflate two of the three stances: the design stance and the intentional stance. In his earlier work, Dennett stresses the difference between these stances: at the design level, we predict and explain a system's behaviour based on what it is designed to do, while at the intentional level, we predict and explain a system's behaviour based on the assumption that it is optimally designed, that it will do what is most rational. Yet, in his discussion of Darwinism, Dennett claims that adaptationism, the assumption that properties of organisms are *designed* to fulfil certain functions, amounts to taking the *intentional* stance towards Mother Nature, i.e., the process of natural selection (IS, pp. 299–300; DDI, pp. 232–3; 237). This conflation of the intentional with the design stance is merely apparent. Dennett's idea is that, before we can take the design stance towards products of natural selection, e.g., animal organs, we must first take the intentional stance towards the process that generated these products. We must understand what Mother Nature's *intentions* were. Otherwise, we cannot establish what biological structures are supposed to do. This is entirely analogous to applying the design stance to artefacts: in order to know what some artefact is designed to do, we must discern the intentions of its designers from the intentional stance (DDI, pp. 229–33).

Given the way natural selection works, Mother Nature always has the same thing in mind: improving the reproductive capacities of different kinds of replicators, principally genes, but lately, in human cultural environments, memes as well. This is precisely the perspective recommended by Dawkins: the gene's 'point of view' (1976). From this perspective, when seeking to understand phenotypic design, we must ask how phenotypic structures contribute to the reproduction of genes or other replicators that code for them.

This perspective enables us to explain examples of *apparently* poor design in nature. As we saw in chapter 2, Stich (1982, p. 52) criticizes Dennett's claim that intentional descriptions presuppose rationality, pointing out that evolved systems, like animals, often act in irrational, e.g., paranoid, ways. Potential prey does not wait to satisfy scientific canons of hypothesis confirmation before concluding that there may be predators present. But, from the gene's point of view, such apparently suboptimal design may be entirely rational: why squander resources on constructing nervous systems capable of following scientific canons of hypothesis confirmation when this is unnecessary and may be harmful given the time constraints on survival in the wild? If the gene's goal is to increase the chances of its own reproduction, cheap mechanisms that are correct enough of the time, and avoid unnecessary risks, are often the most efficient means to this end. In general, as Dennett puts it, quoting Francis Crick, 'evolution is cleverer than you are' (DDI, p. 74), so apparently poor design may always conceal an optimally rational strategy, from the gene's point of view. Thus, taking the intentional stance towards the process of natural selection, by assuming that any phenotype is (close to) an optimal solution to a genotype's problem of replicating in a specific environment, reveals designs that might not otherwise occur to us.

Adaptationism, the assumption that phenotypic traits are designed to fulfil functions, is therefore equivalent to taking the intentional stance towards Mother Nature, or natural selection. The goals we ascribe to genes and other replicators when we take this stance are not *represented* by any mind. They are, in Dennett's terms, 'free floating rationales' (IS, p. 259). These are the reasons behind most apparently intelligent activity and design in the natural world. In fact, much human behaviour, though it may appear non-rational relative to reasons we consciously endorse, is eminently rational relative to the free-floating rationales of our genes and the process that selected them (FE, pp. 260–1). The concept of a free-floating rationale is central to Dennett's solution to the reconciliation problem. Because entirely unintelligent, non-minded mechanisms, like genes and the processes that govern their replication, can have reasons for doing things, and in particular, reasons for building biological structures, minds can be understood as naturally designed artefacts.

However, Dennett's understanding of adaptations and intentional states in terms of free floating rationales raises the question: do adaptations and intentional states really exist? Natural selection is supposed to be the ultimate source of all intentionality and design in the natural world, including human thought. However, if anything has merely 'as if' or metaphorical intentionality, it is natural selection. This is a mechanism with absolutely no foresight, a 'blind watchmaker', to use Dawkins' (1986) phrase. In what sense does natural selection *really* have goals, for example? And if ascribing free-floating rationales to the genes it selects is merely metaphorical, then all intentional states derived from such free-floating rationales, including human thoughts, are no less metaphorical. This is one of the most influential criticisms of Dennett's entire program, and we discussed a version of it in chapter 2. It is the claim that Dennett is nothing but an *instrumentalist*: to him, intentionality and design are nothing but useful conceptual tools; they correspond to nothing real in the natural world. As we saw in chapter 2, Dennett counters that any perspective that ignores intentionality and design in the natural world misses a *real pattern*, and so these concepts are more than of merely instrumental value. Below and in chapter 7, I explore Dennett's notion of a real pattern, with the aim of determining whether it can do all the philosophical work that he wants it to do.

Defending Darwin, Part 1

There are at least two general strategies for criticizing Darwinism. The more common strategy focuses on some particularly elaborate denizen of design space and argues that natural selection *could* never produce it. The second strategy is to concede that natural selection *could* produce many biological phenomena, yet argue that the available evidence suggests that it has not. I discuss this second strategy below. The first strategy is the favoured strategy of many of Darwinism's non-scientific critics; however, some renowned scientists have proposed arguments along these lines as well. Examples of natural design that have been proposed as feats beyond the power of natural selection include:

1. the first organisms to emerge from inanimate matter;
2. altruistic behaviour such as is apparent in social insects as well as in human populations;
3. human consciousness; and
4. human culture and morality.

These different phenomena are alleged to be beyond the power of natural selection for different reasons: (1) the first organisms cannot be products of natural selection because before there are organisms present there are no genes or mechanisms of genetic reproduction; (2) natural selection cannot explain altruistic behaviour because altruists sacrifice resources necessary for survival and reproduction, and hence would not persist in populations over the long run; (3) since we can imagine 'zombie' organisms that behave just as conscious persons do, and hence are just as well adapted, consciousness contributes nothing to survival and reproduction; (4) human culture and morality often recommend behaviour that is obviously counteradaptive, like chastity and sacrificing one's life for another.

Many of these arguments were anticipated and answered by Darwin himself and his intellectual heirs. The basic strategy is to propose elaborations of natural selection that go beyond the original mechanism yet preserve its central insight: that design can be explained as a product of unintelligent, algorithmic processes. In Dennett's terms, responding to such arguments requires the construction of more elaborate cranes. For example, Darwinian explanations of some forms of altruism are now widely accepted as triumphs of Darwinism (Cronin 1991). The key to understanding how such phenomena are possible is the gene-centred perspective recommended by Dawkins. Any phenotypic property that results in a comparatively higher rate of reproduction of genes that code for it will come to dominate a population.

For example, according to Hamilton's concept of 'inclusive fitness' (1964), genes carried by one individual are also carried by others, so when one individual sacrifices resources in order to help other individuals that carry the same genes, from the gene-centred perspective, the behaviour is adaptive. This underwrites the concept of kin-selection: genes that code for mutual aid among kin are selected because kin tend to carry copies of the same genes, so helping one's kin helps one's own genes reproduce (DDI, p. 478). More recently, it has been shown that reciprocal altruism – helping others on condition that they help you at other times – is likely to evolve, under some conditions, even among individuals that show minimal genetic overlap (DDI, p. 479).

In Dennett's terms, such explanations are excellent examples of cranes: elaborations of the basic mechanism of natural selection that account for phenomena that appear to require a skyhook, without sacrificing Darwin's central insight that all design can be explained as the outcome of the algorithmic selection of more successful replicators. We have already discussed some of Dennett's own attempts to construct cranes to account for some of the other phenomena that are alleged to be beyond the power of Darwinian mechanisms. In chapter 4, we discussed his explanation of the evolution of human consciousness. In chapter 5, we discussed his explanation of the evolution of human culture, freedom and morality. The central component of these cranes is the emergence of a new kind of replicator: the meme.

As we have seen, Dawkins' (1976) notion of a meme does a lot of important work for Dennett. Once there are organisms with the cognitive capacity for cultural learning, i.e., the capacity to acquire, what Dennett calls, 'good tricks' from each other, these good tricks acquire a life of their own. Such ideas, or memes, start competing with each other for control of human brains, in a way analogous to the competition between genes for resources required for their replication. Since human brains and media of communication are limited, and memes vary in their capacities to control human brains and be transmitted through media of communication, there is bound to be differential reproduction of memes: some will survive longer and reproduce more than others. In Dennett's terms, these meme-based evolutionary mechanisms are 'cranes of culture' (DDI, p. 335).

Because the means of transmitting most memes, language, can be used to control information flow in the brain through serial, verbal self-stimulation, the virtual Joycean machine is installed, and gives rise to our self-conception as controlled by a centre of narrative gravity that we call the conscious self. This explains the evolution of consciousness: its adaptive role consists in solving the problem of cognitive self-control, which likely faced our ancestors, through a kind of verbal self-discipline (CE).

Furthermore, because memes care primarily for their own replication, and not for the replication of the genes that construct their human hosts, it is no surprise that cultural and moral phenomena, like abstinence and self-sacrifice, arise in human populations. The meme for abstinence can spread through cultural intercourse, even if many individuals animated by this meme fail to reproduce their genes through sexual intercourse. The meme for self-sacrifice can likewise spread through cultural intercourse, even if many individuals animated by this meme die before reproducing biologically. In addition, as we saw in chapter 5, the specific, ecological circumstances of our hominid precursors likely selected for memes that encouraged conformity to communal norms, and resistance to short-term temptations to cheat. The success of our species is largely due to our ability to cooperate, by transcending the short-sighted self-interest that leads to prisoner's dilemmas. It is no surprise that, in such circumstances, such apparently counteradaptive memes as self-sacrifice and abstinence have spread. Dennett devotes his latest book, *Breaking the Spell: Religion as a Natural Phenomenon* (2006), to explaining the diverse religious traditions and rituals that characterize human populations, in terms of why certain memes are selected and persist.

Dennett also devotes substantial energy to exploring cranes capable of explaining the evolution of the first life forms from inanimate precursors (DDI, pp. 155–63). The emergence of the first life forms poses a problem for Darwinism because natural selection *presupposes* a lot of design, including, most importantly, the machinery responsible for the construction and replication of genes. Such machinery is *part* of the living world so, before there were any life forms, it did not exist. But, Dennett argues, following Küppers (1990) and Eigen (1992), prior to the evolution of gene-based life forms, natural selection likely operated on far simpler structures, yielding a kind of 'molecular evolution' (DDI, p. 155), that eventually led to DNA, and all the other machinery on which contemporary life-forms rely to build and replicate genes.

Thus, Dennett and others have proposed imaginative variants on the basic Darwinian insight to construct cranes capable of lifting organisms to areas of design space that critics claim are inaccessible to such mechanisms. I turn now to the second strategy for criticizing Darwinism: the claim, made famous by Gould and collaborators that, whether or not natural selection *could* give rise to most biological phenomena, as a matter of fact, the evidence is that it has not.

Defending Darwin, Part 2

Gould and collaborators claim that there is considerable anatomical and palaeontological evidence that, as a matter of fact, most important biological phenomena are not products of natural selection (Gould and Eldredge 1993; Gould and Lewontin 1979; Gould and Vrba 1981). First, the Darwinist embrace of natural selection drastically underestimates the degree to which hidden physical or architectural constraints, on the development of phenotypes from genotypes, constrain which regions of design space are accessible. Second, Darwinism falsely assumes that evolution, and, in particular, *speciation*,[3] are the result of the *gradual* accumulation of adaptive mutations. On the contrary, the fossil record shows long periods of equilibrium punctuated by dramatic 'saltations' (DDI, pp. 285–9), or leaps that yield new species.

Dennett does not dispute the *substance* of most of Gould's proposals; rather, he questions their *significance*. He sees them as minor correctives to Darwinism. What Dennett objects to is the inflated, revolutionary rhetoric that accompanies many of Gould's proposals (DDI, p. 278). This rhetoric has led many contemporary intellectuals to assume that Darwinism is bankrupt. A closer examination of Gould's actual proposals shows that they are entirely consistent with Darwinism, and in many cases, explicitly endorsed by Darwinists.

Consider the first issue: hidden architectural constraints on development may significantly restrict the accessibility of regions in design space to natural selection. Gould and Lewontin's (1979) flagship analogy for such hidden constraints in evolution are the repeated, symmetrically placed spandrels supporting the dome of San Marco Cathedral, in Venice. These spandrels, called pendentives, appear deliberately designed. However, argue Gould and Lewontin, this is an illusion: they are actually 'necessary architectural by-products of mounting a dome on rounded arches' (DDI, p. 271). According to Gould and Lewontin, many biological structures are like such spandrels: though they seem designed, they are just by-products of inevitable architectural constraints on the construction of living organisms.[4]

Even if many biological structures result from hidden constraints on 'constructing' organisms, rather than from natural selection, Dennett argues that this does not confute Darwinian adaptationism (DDI, pp. 257–61). Adaptationists conceive of evolution as the gradual discovery of solutions to problems related to the reproduction of genes in specific environments. Obviously, physical features of those environments constrain possible solutions. Among those physical features are substances and structures involved in the development of phenotypes from genotypes. Genes can only replicate if they code for phenotypes that can develop to reproductive maturity, so adaptation to architecturally necessary features of development is to be expected from a Darwinian perspective. It is possible that limited knowledge of such architectural constraints leads adaptationists to overestimate the diversity of designs accessible to natural selection, but, as Dennett puts it, 'the discovery of such constraints ... [is] an integral part of (good) adaptationist reasoning' (DDI, p. 270). In fact, as Dennett argues, it is hard to see how one might discover architectural constraints on development without engaging in adaptationist reasoning (DDI, p. 257). The only way to tell whether a trait is an inevitable by-product of development, rather than an adaptation, is to show that it is non-adaptive. But one can only do this by engaging in adaptationist reasoning: one determines what the trait *should* be, on adaptationist grounds, and shows that the actual trait does not live up to this ideal.

Even if many biological structures originate as non-functional by-products of hidden architectural constraints, Gould admits that they may later be put to uses related to enhancing the reproduction of genes. This is Gould's notion of an 'exaptation' – putting a structure that had no function, or a different function, to a new use (Gould and Vrba 1981). But exaptations are hardly embarrassments for Darwinian adaptationism. As Dennett writes, 'according to orthodox Darwinism, every adaptation is one sort of exaptation or ... other ... if you go back far enough, you will find that every adaptation has developed out of predecessor structures each of which either had some other use or no use at all' (DDI, p. 281). As Dennett never tires of pointing out, natural selection is an opportunistic tinkerer, retooling available materials just enough to make a difference to the reproduction of genes (CE, p. 175; DDI, pp. 225–6). No Darwinian claims that every biological trait is adaptive (panadaptationism), or that all currently adaptive traits were originally selected for some adaptive function (preadaptationism) (DDI, pp. 277–81). So Gould's proposals are, to use Dennett's words, 'reforms or complications, not revolutions'

(DDI, p. 278). Disagreements between Gould and Darwinians amount to differences over the relative importance of natural selection. However, the rhetoric of Gould and his collaborators belies these relatively modest differences: many take their work to signal the demise of Darwinism (DDI, p. 278).

Gould's other main argument against Darwinism targets its *gradualist* assumptions. Natural selection is supposed to explain evolution and speciation in terms of the gradual accumulation of incremental adaptations: focused, minimal solutions to specific problems related to the reproduction of genomes in specific environments. However, Gould claims that the fossil record contradicts this hypothesis (Gould and Eldredge 1993). Rather than a gradual replacement of new forms by old forms, through many intermediate forms, the fossil record shows long periods of equilibrium or stasis punctuated by the sudden emergence of new species.

Dennett responds that this argument largely trades on a confusion of scale. A period which seems sudden at geological timescales may be long enough for gradual adaptation to take place. The temporal resolution of the fossil record is such that gradual evolution through intermediate forms, if it takes less than millions of years, is likely to be invisible. This does not mean that it did not take place. As Dawkins (1986, p. 242) demonstrates, drawing on a thought experiment by Stebbins, a gradual process of evolution lasting sixty thousand years, in which a mouse-sized mammal is subjected to a constant selection pressure for increased size, which remains invisible relative to human lifespans, would yield an elephant-sized mammal. Sixty thousand years is regarded as geologically instantaneous, because it is too short to be measured by ordinary methods for dating the fossil record (DDI, p. 292). Thus, the fact that the fossil record shows periods of equilibrium punctuated by dramatic changes does not confute Darwinian gradualism.

As Dennett points out, gradualism is not the same as what Dawkins calls 'constant speedism' (DDI, p. 290; Dawkins 1986, p. 244). Evolution might proceed through gradual accumulations of mutations, but this process might occur at different rates, at different times. This is not at odds with Darwinism; in fact, Darwin himself endorsed this view (Darwin 1959, p. 727). There are good Darwinian reasons to expect evolution to proceed through punctuated equilibria. First, speciation is bound to have this structure, since we would not call something a species that had not persisted for a significant amount of time. So the emergence of new species from old must appear as punctuations of long periods of equilibrium (DDI, p. 293). Furthermore, there is a good Darwinian explanation for this. Most modifications of a successful suite of adaptations are likely to be counteradaptive. If some phenotype has worked well in a particular niche, then any random variant on it, caused by mutation, is likely to die out quickly. Natural selection is often a conservative process, preserving what works over constantly generated random variants (DDI, p. 293). It is only in rare and comparatively brief periods, where selection pressures change so dramatically that some mutant has a sudden advantage, that natural selection favours innovation.

Thus, according to Dennett, for all of their rhetorical bluster, Gould and his collaborators fail to refute Darwinism. On the contrary, they make important contributions to the Darwinian paradigm, by pointing out that the effects of hidden constraints, exaptations and punctuated equilibria on evolution are often underestimated. But none of these phenomena are incompatible with natural selection. In fact, as Dennett points out, exaptation and punctuated equilibria can be explained as inevitable consequences of natural selection. And hidden constraints are only revealed relative to the default assumption that natural selection yields phenotypes designed to reproduce genotypes as effectively as possible in specific environments.

Real patterns

Dennett's defence of Darwinism and, indeed, his entire philosophical system, rest on a very specific, very simple and very controversial proposal. We explored this proposal in chapter 2, and Dennett has defended it since his earliest writings. The proposal is that any system, no matter how simple, that is reliably and voluminously predictable via the ascription of intentional states, has genuine intentionality. In other words, any system the behaviour of which we can make sense of by ascribing goals and access to information about the world, and therefore, reasons to do things, *really* has goals, access to information about the world and reasons to do things. This proposal underwrites Dennett's assimilation of evolved to artificial intelligence, his defence of adaptationism in biology and his non-reductive reconciliation of the manifest with the scientific images. As we saw in chapters 2 through 5, other manifest concepts – like consciousness, personhood and freedom – are understood in terms of different kinds of intentional states. For this reason, Dennett's whole approach to the reconciliation problem depends on the idea that physical systems as simple and mechanical as genes can have *genuine* intentionality, in virtue of the fact that the ascription of intentional states to them is explanatorily useful.

On the face of it, this seems like an implausible claim. There appears to be all the difference in the world between systems, like human beings, that *really* have goals, access to information and reasons for doing things, and systems, like thermostats, to which it is merely sometimes *useful* to ascribe such intentional states. As Dennett often points out (BS 9), human beings are prone to anthropomorphism – projecting human characteristics onto inanimate phenomena. He himself gives a particularly extreme example: an electrician might speak of lightning 'wanting' to find the shortest path to the ground (IS, p. 22). In chapter 2, we saw that a common criticism of Dennett is that he conflates such merely useful, non-literal ways of speaking, with *true* intentionality. This leads to the charge of *instrumentalism*, the view that manifest concepts like intentionality are merely useful, and correspond to nothing real in the world as science describes it.

As we saw in chapter 2, one way of appreciating this worry is to consider a hypothetical scientist, a Martian say, with far greater computational powers than any human scientist. To this Martian, human beings appear as simple as thermostats. It would not be useful to this Martian to understand our behaviour in intentional terms, because they could just as easily understand it in physical terms. If all it is for a system to have intentional states is the fact that some scientist finds it useful to ascribe them to the system, then, relative to the Martian, human beings would not have intentional states. This is troublesome not just because, potentially, it robs human beings of their minds. The main problem is that it makes having intentional states, and therefore all the mental phenomena that depend on them, *perspective-dependent*. Whether or not you, or I, or any system has intentional states, on this view, is not an *objective fact*; rather, it depends on who is doing the describing and for what purpose.

Dennett's response to this worry invokes the notion of a 'real pattern'. Any scientist or thinker that explained human behaviour without ascribing intentional states would be missing a real pattern in the data. Intentionality is not in the eye of the beholder because the behaviour of any intentional system follows a pattern that is really there, whether or not anyone chooses to see it by adopting the intentional stance towards the system. So Dennett's response to the charge of instrumentalism depends on whether this notion of a real pattern can be understood precisely and defended. Given that the charge of instrumentalism strikes at the heart of his entire philosophical system, this is a crucial issue. Dennett addresses it in an important paper called 'Real Patterns' (BC, pp. 95–120).

Drawing on work in algorithmic information theory (Chaitin 1975), Dennett offers the following definition of a real pattern. A real pattern exists in some data if it is possible to *compress* the data. Consider the following 'bit-string':[5] 1010101010101010. Suppose you want to inform someone that this is the output of some program on a computer. You can either send the string verbatim, or you can summarize it as ' "10" repeated 8 times'. Assuming that the latter description can be coded using fewer bits, it constitutes a compression of the data. Random bit-strings, like 10111010110010001, cannot be compressed. According to Dennett, if a set of data cannot be compressed, then it does not contain a real pattern.

Given this definition, Dennett can defend a kind of realism about intentional states. On his view, a system *really* has intentional states if a physical level description of its behaviour can be compressed using an intentional level description. Take for example a chess-playing computer. Imagine the physical description of every state the computer goes through during a game. This would constitute an incredibly large set of 'raw' data: every change in electrical potential across any circuit, every key press, every change on the monitor, from the opening move to the final mate, would have to be recorded, but all that is important in this data could be expressed in a relatively brief intentional level description. For example, one could say that the program *thought* you were executing a king's gambit and *decided* to open with a Falkbeer counter gambit, etc. Because the physically described data can be compressed via the ascription of intentional states, the intentional stance enables us to track a real pattern in the data. Since, as we have seen, ascribing intentional states to humans and other living systems, as well as to genes and natural selection, enables even greater compression of data, the intentional stance reveals real patterns in all of these phenomena and so, according to Dennett, they all count as genuinely intentional.

The definition of real pattern proposed by Dennett implies that the alleged distinction between what is really the case and what is in the eye of the beholder assumes a false alternative. A pattern can really exist in the data, yet only be visible from certain perspectives. Indeed different individuals of the same kind, e.g., different human beings, can choose to track different real patterns that exist in the same set of data, depending on their purposes, abilities and tolerance for error.

For example, when playing chess against a computer, you must track the intentional patterns in its behaviour. You understand it as *trying* to mate you, *anticipating* your counter gambits, etc. Although this assumption of the intentional stance enables you to save a lot of time and energy, as we saw in chapter 2, it is *risky*. There may be a bug in the computer's program, or the hardware might fail, or the program might not be optimally designed to deal with certain chess strategies. In such cases, expectations based on assuming the intentional stance may fail. According to Dennett, this shows that the real pattern tracked from the intentional stance is *noisy*: sometimes the data does not fit the pattern (BC, pp.100–04). However, the intentional pattern is still real, because the assumption of the intentional stance still accomplishes impressive data compression. An intentional description, together with a list of unexpected errors or noise, may still constitute a substantial compression of the information in a physical description. In the case of playing a good chess program, the information compression achieved by assuming the intentional stance is usually worth the risk of occasional noise.

On the other hand, if you are a programmer assessing the performance of the very same chess program in the very same game, you might need to track a different real pattern in the same data. Suppose you are interested in whether or not the program's different subroutines are executing properly. Then you need to track the program's behaviour from the design stance. You see the program's moves not as attempts to win a game of chess, but rather as executions of different bits of code that you have written. This pattern is less economical than the intentional pattern: there is less information compression because you need to keep track of all the algorithmic details of the program the computer is executing. For this reason, there is less risk. Behaviour that counts as noise from the intentional stance fits into the pattern tracked from the design stance. For example, a non-optimal response to a type of chess strategy counts as noise relative to the intentional stance, but may be expected from the design stance: perhaps it was just not worth including a subroutine for dealing with such a rarely used strategy, so, from the program-or design-level stance, the optimal response is not part of the expected pattern. Both the riskier yet more economical intentional pattern and the less risky yet more expensive design pattern really exist in the data, but which pattern one decides to track depends on one's purposes and capacities.

Dennett dramatizes this point even further by appealing to a computer simulation known as the Game of Life. The Game of Life is a simulation of a very simple universe, a very simple version of such computer games as SimWorld. This simulation plays a very important role in Dennett's later thought. He uses it to explain his notion of a real pattern (BC, pp. 105–10), to demonstrate how design might emerge in worlds with regular laws (DDI, pp. 166–76), and to show that evitability is compatible with determinism (FE, pp. 36–47). So impressed is Dennett with the philosophical implications of the Game of Life that he recommends that 'every philosophy student should be held responsible for an intimate acquaintance with [it] ... It should be considered an essential tool in every thought-experimenter's kit, a prodigiously versatile generator of philosophically important examples and thought experiments of admirable clarity and vividness' (BC, p. 105).

The Game of Life is played on a two-dimensional grid, like a piece of graph paper. There are sophisticated, computerized versions of it, some of which you can explore on the Internet.[6] Here I will only explain the rules of the game very briefly, restricting myself to a paper-and-pencil version of the game.[7] Take a pencil and shade in a few squares on a piece of graph paper at random. Each square (except those at the edge of the page) has eight neighbours, and can be in one of two states – shaded or clear. Go to the first square and look at its eight neighbours. If two of its neighbours are shaded, the square stays in whatever state it is in. If three of its neighbours are shaded, the square must be shaded. If less than two, or more than three of its neighbours are shaded, then the square must be clear. Repeat for all squares. Following these rules likely causes a change in the initial, randomly chosen pattern of shaded squares. Continue applying these rules to the entire grid, in discrete time steps or turns. The pattern of shaded squares should evolve.

These simple rules constitute the lowest level, 'physical stance' understanding of the Game of Life world. When you apply them to any randomly chosen pattern of shaded squares, you are able to predict, with utmost precision, the sequence of future patterns that will evolve from this initial pattern. To use a term introduced in the discussion of determinism, in chapter 5, when you play the Game of Life, you have the powers of a Laplacean demon. You have perfect knowledge of the physical laws governing any possible physical state of the Life World, and this enables you to predict every future physical state. However, as Dennett points out, if this is all you think is going on in the Game of Life, then you are missing extremely significant real patterns. Just as the Martian scientist who tracks human behaviour entirely based on the laws governing our physical components misses real patterns available from the intentional stance, if you restrict yourself to the basic, lowest-level rules of the Game of Life, you will miss real patterns visible from higher-level, design-like stances.

Consider the following pattern of shaded squares on the Game of Life plane.

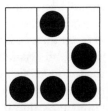

If you apply the rules to this pattern, it will displace itself down the grid in four turns. For this reason, the pattern is called a 'glider'. In computer simulations that apply the rules of the Game of Life at fast speeds, such patterns appear to glide across the grid. The effect is compelling and dramatic. Looking at this pattern for several dozen generations, it is impossible to escape the impression that it is moving across the plane of the Game of Life world. But this pattern is invisible from the lowest level stance, from which only shaded and clear squares, to which the basic rules are applied, are visible. At the lowest level, there is no motion. Individual squares are shaded or clear, but none of them move. This raises, in a very compelling way, Dennett's questions regarding real patterns. We can predict the evolution of the glider pattern with perfect precision from the lowest level, restricting our attention to the shading and clearing of individual squares, according to the basic rules of the Game of Life. Yet, despite this, it is impossible to escape the impression that, if we restrict ourselves to this level of description, we miss something very important. Gliders are real, and they really move!

Gliders are among the simplest denizens of the Game of Life. Researchers have uncovered hundreds of other higher-level structures, with interesting higher-level properties that remain invisible at the level of individual squares being shaded and cleared according to the basic rules. For example, there are glider guns, capable of generating streams of gliders, oscillators, still lifes, spaceships and puffer trains.[8] In order to notice such higher-level patterns, it is necessary to adopt a higher-level stance.

According to Dennett, the difference between seeing a glider as a set of squares being shaded or cleared according to the basic rules, and seeing it as a single structure, gliding across the grid, is like the difference between describing an artefact or organism from the physical stance, and describing it from the design stance. The lower level stance buys you perfect precision. Because the Game of Life is governed by the same basic set of rules indefinitely, by applying these rules you are guaranteed to know exactly which squares will be shaded and which will be cleared indefinitely. But this is a very time- and resource-consuming process. For larger grids, calculating the future state of every square becomes prohibitively time-consuming for human beings. Think of all the time you save when you see the glider pattern *as a glider*, and predict that it will glide downward. By tracking this real pattern, Dennett argues that you gain tremendous predictive power, thanks to tremendous savings in computational costs.

Furthermore, just as in the case of adopting the design stance towards artefacts and organisms, adopting the higher level glider stance towards the Game of Life is *risky*. The design stance assumes that artefacts and organisms behave as designed, but this assumption can fail if enabling physical conditions are not present. An alarm clock hit with a hammer will likely fail to work as designed. Similarly, if a glider 'hits' a region of the grid that is occupied by other shaded squares, it will likely disintegrate. You can predict that the glider will move in one direction indefinitely, on condition that it does not encounter other shaded squares, in which case the basic rules of the life world can be used to predict that the glider will disintegrate. Just as in real life, when expectations formed at higher levels are thwarted due to physical glitches, such behaviour must be explained at the lower-level, physical stance.

The Game of Life offers opportunities for intentional stance descriptions as well. As Dennett notes, researchers have proven that a Universal Turing Machine can be constructed out of the denizens of the Game of Life, including gliders, glider-guns and other structures. As we saw in chapter 4, a Universal Turing Machine is capable of executing any algorithmically specifiable procedure. It is because they approximate Universal Turing

Machines that digital computers can run programs, like chess players. Therefore, since a Universal Turing Machine can be constructed in the Game of Life world, so can a chess player. As we saw in chapter 2, on Dennett's view, chess-playing programs are intentional systems: we can adopt the intentional stance towards them, i.e., treat them as *wanting* to checkmate us, *fearing* our gambits, *plotting* counter gambits, etc. It follows that some structures in the Game of Life world count as intentional systems as well. A grid capable of running a Game of Life simulation of a chess-playing program would be enormous: Dennett estimates it would be a kilometre across, if pixels turning 'on' and 'off' replace shaded and clear squares and we assume the resolution of pixels on a standard laptop computer (DDI, pp. 171–3; FE, p. 49, fn. 3). There is no way that we could, in realistic time, track the evolution of such enormous patterns by applying the basic rules of the Game of Life to the switching on and off of all of these pixels. But an intentional stance description, that treats the configuration as a chess player trying to win a game of chess, suddenly makes the flurry of activity on this enormous grid predictable and explicable.

According to Dennett, adaptationism in biology, the ascription of intentional states in psychology, and the application of manifest concepts like freedom, personhood and consciousness in everyday life, are precisely analogous to the application of higher levels of description in the Game of Life. Researchers would not have been able to prove that a Universal Turing Machine can be constructed in the Game of Life world had they not availed themselves of concepts like glider and glider gun. In the same way, biologists would miss comparably indispensable real patterns if they did not assume that biological structures are adaptive, i.e., designed by natural selection to help the replication of genes that code for them. Psychologists would miss comparably indispensable real patterns if they did not assume that humans and other animals engage in rational behaviour, aimed at satisfying desires, in the light of beliefs they have about the world. And persons would miss comparably indispensable real patterns if we did not treat others as freely deciding on courses of action, in the light of consciously contemplated beliefs and desires.

Dennett provides a rhetorically compelling defence of the idea that patterns discernible from the intentional stance are real, grounded in a precise definition of what a real pattern is. He is correct that anyone who treated human beings, organisms and many artefacts as purely physical systems, with no goals or access to information, would miss a real pattern in their behaviour, whether or not she could predict this behaviour perfectly. However, it is unclear whether Dennett's proposal adequately responds to the charge of instrumentalism. As Churchland notes (1989, p. 126), many false scientific theories track real patterns in the data. When one is navigating on the open water, it is often easiest to assume the geocentric stance towards planets and stars. Assuming that the earth is at the centre of the universe and that celestial bodies move around it permits tremendous savings of time and computational resources, and tracks a real pattern. After all, you can get rich betting that the sun will *rise* every morning, on the grounds that it moves around the earth. The geocentric pattern is real, but systematically misleading. Churchland complains that Dennett provides no reason against a similar verdict regarding the intentional patterns discernible in the behaviour of genes, organisms, artefacts and human beings.

I think that Dennett's view has the resources to answer this objection. The intentional pattern is grounded in an objectively real, concrete, physical phenomenon: replicators subject to natural selection. Once such physical structures are present, intentional patterns are bound to emerge. Next, in the concluding chapter, I discuss this objection and response, together with others, in greater detail.

Chapter Seven

Dennett's 'synoptic' vision
problems and prospects

Preamble

As we saw in chapter 1, Dennett's project is, in broadest terms, an attempt to reconcile what the American philosopher Wilfrid Sellars called the manifest and scientific images of human beings. Sellars asks: 'To what extent does manifest man survive in the synoptic view which does equal justice to the scientific image which now confronts us?' (Sellars 1963, p. 15). In this concluding chapter, I pose this question for Dennett's synoptic vision. In particular, I briefly survey different objections that have been raised against Dennett's proposed solution to the problem of reconciling the scientific with the manifest image of human beings. Most of these express scepticism concerning whether the most important components of the manifest image survive in Dennett's synoptic vision. I also discuss other potential problems with Dennett's proposals, as well as prospects for persuasive responses to these criticisms. But before I turn to this, I survey Dennett's system, as well as its central assumptions, themes and methods.

The Dennettian system

This section's title has an odd ring to it. Dennett is often accused of, and cheerfully acknowledges, a lack of concern with philosophical system-building (Ross 2000). However, as I hope chapters 2 through 6 have shown, beneath Dennett's casual and explorative expository style lies a deeply coherent and ambitious philosophical system, founded on a small number of clear and consistently applied metaphysical and methodological principles.

Here is how Dennett characterizes his own project:

> My project ... is to demonstrate how a standard, normal respect for science – *Time Magazine* standard, nothing more doctrinaire – leads inexorably to my views about consciousness, intentionality, free will, and so forth. I view science not as an unquestionable foundation, but simply as a natural ally of my philosophical claims that most philosophers and scientists would be reluctant to oppose. My 'scientism' comes in the form of a package deal: you think you can have your everyday science and reject my 'behaviourism' as too radical? Think again.
>
> (Dennett 1993, p. 205)

This short quotation encapsulates many of the themes that I have emphasized throughout the previous chapters. His clear goal is to reconcile science with concepts like consciousness, intentionality and free will. He appeals to uncontroversial science – the '*Time Magazine* standard' that 'most philosophers and scientists would be reluctant to oppose'. Thus, his starting point is not controversial. However, although many philosophers accept his starting point, the majority refuse to accept the implications he draws from it.

As Dennett appears to acknowledge in this quotation, much of this resistance derives from scepticism about his philosophical 'behaviourism'. He puts this word in scare-quotes because he does not think that his views are guilty of the excesses of traditional philosophical behaviourism. However, this term does label a strong current in his thought, a current that derives from his teacher, Gilbert Ryle. As we saw in chapter 1, philosophical or logical behaviourism, in its most crass form, is the attempt to analyse manifest concepts in terms of dispositions to publicly observable behaviour. This project was inspired by the work of Ryle and others who claimed that the reconciliation problem arises from the misapplication of manifest concepts to domains in which they do not belong. Manifest concepts apply to observable patterns of behaviour in which whole persons and organisms engage, not to causal mechanisms hidden in brains.

Although Dennett does not endorse extreme philosophical behaviourism – the view that all manifest concepts can be *defined* in terms of dispositions to publicly observable behaviour – we have seen that he has great sympathy for the general Rylean strategy. He diagnoses the misleading metaphor of the Cartesian Theatre (CE, p. 17), and its scientific offspring, Cartesian Materialism (CE, p. 107), as arising from a category mistake: the misapplication of the distinction between the observed and the yet-to-be-observed to processes within an individual's nervous system. Philosophers and scientists who make the conscious self so 'small' (FE, pp. 122, 242) that it can play no role in initiating actions are guilty of a comparable category mistake: again, a concept, the application of which makes perfect sense at scales involving whole persons, is misapplied to the microscopic scales of individual brains. In general, as we have seen in the previous chapters, the behaviourist strategy of deflating manifest concepts plays an important role in Dennett's proposed solution to the reconciliation problem. If manifest concepts apply primarily to observable patterns of behaviour in which whole persons and organisms engage, rather than to causal mechanisms hidden within individuals, then they are far easier to reconcile with the scientific image. No matter what science discovers about how our brains function, it remains the case that we do engage in observable patterns of behaviour that can be tracked through the application of manifest concepts.

However, Dennett's use of the behaviourist strategy is more careful than Ryle's. Unlike classical philosophical behaviourists, he is not interested in doing justice to ordinary concepts. Rather, he is interested in *revising* manifest concepts with a view to making them easier to integrate with the scientific image. Classical philosophical behaviourists had no concern for the scientific image. Dennett, on the other hand, uses a *neo-behaviourist* strategy – providing *revisionist* definitions of manifest concepts in terms of publicly observable patterns of behaviour – to reconcile the manifest with the scientific images. The concept of an intentional system is deliberately purged of the trappings of the ordinary concept of a believer, which, according to Dennett, are at odds with what standard science tells us about the world. The method of heterophenomenology is deliberately purged of the trappings of phenomenology, which, according to Dennett, are at odds with what standard science tells us about the world. And then Dennett makes his controversial move: if one accepts that standard, '*Time Magazine*' science describes all there is in the world, then one must hold that, insofar as manifest concepts apply to objects in the world, they are exhausted by the revisionary, surrogate, behaviourist concepts that Dennett invents. If believers exist then, given what science tells us, they must be nothing more than intentional systems. If phenomenology is real then, given what science tells us, it must be exhaustively captured using heterophenomenology.

This is Dennettian 'bait and switch' (DDI, p. 214), a strategy inspired by natural selection. Just as natural selection often *seems* to solve one very difficult problem, while actually faking it by solving different, easier problems, Dennett proposes to solve the traditional reconciliation problem by inventing replacement manifest concepts that are easier to reconcile with the scientific image. But, according to Dennett, such pragmatic opportunism is entirely justified if the truth of standard science is one of one's core assumptions. His claim is conditional: if one accepts standard science, then these are the only viable versions of manifest concepts.

Dennett's methodological commitment to respect for standard science leads him to endorse, sometimes only implicitly, sometimes explicitly, a small set of core metaphysical assumptions. First, as we have seen in the previous chapters, intelligence cannot be an unexplained explainer. Intelligence and design can only be explained in terms of non-intelligent, mechanical, algorithmic processes. There is no room for intelligent homunculi in the brain or for skyhooks in evolution. Dennett's metaphysical commitment to mechanism goes hand in hand with his methodological abhorrence of mystery. Both explain his focus on AI and Darwinian biology as points of contact between the manifest and the scientific images.

Dennett's commitment to mechanism should not be confused with an endorsement of reductionism. His second core metaphysical assumption is a *kind* of non-reductionism. In his earlier work, Dennett stresses that his proposals are not reductionist. For example, he refuses to identify intentional phenomena with either neurophysiological or computational mechanisms (BS, p. xix; IS, pp. 66–7). These early claims appear to be in tension with his later rhetoric. The books he has published in the last fifteen years, aimed at a popular audience, are taken by many to advocate reductionism (SD, pp. 70–71, 145–6). For example, his theory of consciousness seems completely reductionistic: Dennett *identifies* human consciousness with a '"von Neumannesque" virtual machine *implemented* in the *parallel architecture* of a brain' (CE, p. 210): 'Anyone or anything that has such a virtual machine as its control system is conscious in the fullest sense, and is conscious *because* it has such a virtual machine' (CE, p. 281). He even acknowledges this as a reductionistic theory, and defends this reductionism on the grounds that true explanations must leave out what is explained; otherwise they are not explaining it (CE, pp. 454–5; SD, p. 144). But, as he notes in *Darwin's Dangerous Idea*, there is a distinction between good and 'greedy' reductionism (DDI, pp. 82–83). Good reductionism is just the abhorrence of mystery and commitment to mechanism discussed above. Greedy reductionism is the claim that all that really exists can be represented using our lowest-level science, microphysics.

How are we to understand this vacillation? In the philosophical sense, Dennett remains a non-reductionist, at least with regard to intentionality.[1] This is because he refuses to *identify* intentional phenomena with any variety of lower-level phenomena. This is the point of his notion of real patterns. Reality is stratified, and the different levels are largely independent of each other in the following sense: concepts appropriate to one level are insufficient for explaining or understanding other levels. However, this does not mean that lower-level concepts play no role in explaining higher level concepts. Clearly, for Dennett, the mechanical phenomena to which AI and Darwinian biology appeal contribute to such explanations. But such explanatory contributions do not depend on identification: it is not in virtue of being *identical* with an intentional phenomenon that some mechanism explains it. Rather, it is in virtue of giving rise to real patterns that can be tracked only from the intentional stance that a mechanism explains some intentional phenomenon.

The problem with greedy reductionism is that, at least in some forms, it violates a third metaphysical assumption that, as we have seen, Dennett endorses: anti-essentialism. On many views, in order to identify intentionality with some mechanistic property, it is first necessary to define it precisely: to identify the essence of the intentional. But, as we have seen, Dennett thinks this is incompatible with a Darwinian world. Because biological forms evolve gradually from other biological forms, there are no clear lines demarcating biological phenomena. Since intentionality is a biological phenomenon, the application conditions of this concept are indeterminate as well. This is why we cannot *identify* intentionality with any mechanism. We must identify it in terms of our own dispositions to apply intentional concepts. These gradually grade off as mechanisms become simpler and less sensitive to information (IS, pp. 29–33). Intentionality is explained mechanistically when a mechanical process capable of producing increasingly complex physical systems, to which we are increasingly tempted to apply intentional concepts, is identified. Natural selection is precisely such a process: it shows how systems that succumb to intentional description, with increasing ease, might gradually emerge in the world. Here we have a mechanistic explanation of intentionality that avoids the strict identification of intentional with mechanical properties demanded by greedy reductionism.

This then constitutes Dennett's philosophical system. The phenomena tracked by the manifest image are real, but they are not exactly what we thought them to be. A mystery-free explanation of these phenomena must appeal to unintelligent mechanisms, like computational algorithms and natural selection. But because of how such mechanisms operate, the strict reduction of manifest to scientific concepts is impossible. Natural selection produces categories that gradually grade into each other, so strict demarcation in terms of essences is impossible. This precludes strict reductionism.

All that we can do is explain how mechanisms like natural selection give rise to real patterns that can only be tracked using higher levels of description, like the intentional stance. So the reconciliation problem is solved by (1) revising manifest concepts in a way that makes them more compatible with science, and (2) explaining how algorithmic mechanisms, and especially natural selection, give rise to systems the behaviour of which can only be tracked using revised manifest concepts. Chapters 2 through 6 have provided the details of this general strategy.

Before moving on to consider weaknesses in Dennett's system, and prospects for improvement, I want to make one further note concerning his methodology. Instead of offering precise definitions and formally valid arguments, Dennett relies heavily on brief, pithy parables meant to illustrate the reasons for his views. These parables often rely on conceits drawn from science fiction. Yet Dennett takes them to reveal deep insights into our common-sense conception of the mind, and its compatibility with the sciences of human nature. According to Dennett, many apparently insoluble philosophical problems are really just failures of imagination. Philosophers' minds are captured by suites of metaphors and ways of thinking and speaking that trap them in conceptual corners. These are easily escaped, however, once these metaphors and ways of thinking and speaking lose their grip. The apparent incompatibility between the manifest and scientific images is an example of such a conceptual trap.

Dennett sees himself as offering alternative metaphors, stories and ways of thinking and speaking that can free us from such conceptual dead ends. To use Dennett's own metaphorical understanding of consciousness, the minds of many contemporary philosophers of mind are parasitized by pernicious memes. These memes are very good at getting themselves reproduced in other philosophers' or philosophy students' minds. But they are not very useful tools for understanding our place in the world as described by science. As Dennett notes, standard philosophical methods are close to useless for his purposes. He acknowledges that much of what he claims can be refuted by appeal to standard philosophical assumptions. His goal is to shake us free of many of these assumptions (CE, pp. 16–17; FE, p. 307). This cannot be done by argument alone, as arguments are only as effective as the assumptions to which they appeal.

Shoring up chinks in the system

The most pervasive criticisms of Dennett's system are variations on one theme: critics allege that he is changing the subject. For example, the most common complaint about his theory of consciousness is that it is not really a theory of consciousness (Block 1993; Searle 1995). Rather than explaining consciousness, it is alleged, Dennett explains it away. Similar claims have been made about Dennett's accounts of other manifest concepts: intentional systems are not *real* believers; the capacity for flexible self-redesign is not *true* freedom (Strawson 2003). On one interpretation of these complaints, they either miss Dennett's point, or beg the question against him. Dennett is fully aware that the versions of manifest concepts that he attempts to reconcile with the scientific image are revisions of traditional, philosophical versions of these concepts. But his point is that, if we accept standard science, the traditional versions must be revised.

Is this changing the subject? Not any more than conceiving of water as composed of invisible particles changed the subject. When science discovered that water is a substance composed of H_2O molecules, we did not conclude that water does not really exist; rather we concluded that we had been wrong about what water is. Dennett thinks that, if we accept standard science, we must admit similar errors regarding manifest concepts. But this is not the same as saying that intentionality, or consciousness, or freedom are not real. According to Dennett, they are real, but many of the things we have thought about them are false. We can revise our ideas about a topic without changing the subject, and this is precisely what Dennett proposes.

The only responsible way of making the charge of changing the subject stick is to show that Dennett's proposed revisions of manifest concepts are *illegitimate*. Here, one can either argue that there are better revisions available, or that no revision is necessary, or that there are other grounds for rejecting Dennett's proposed revisions. Dennett welcomes the first kind of criticism, and the second is implausible: it amounts to the claim that there is no mind/body or reconciliation problem. Most of Dennett's philosophical critics have focused on the third kind of criticism. Dennett's proposed revisions to manifest concepts, it is argued, are too radical. They throw the baby out with the bathwater. To put it in Sellars' terms, the most important elements of the manifest image do not survive in Dennett's synoptic vision.

Critics have focused on two features, which they claim are central to the manifest image, that do not survive Dennett's revisions of manifest concepts: qualia and the causal powers of intentional states. For the most part, these complaints are supported by appeal to intuitions about the centrality of these concepts to the manifest image. However, the critics who make them also offer supplementary arguments. Both his scepticism about qualia and about the role of intentional states in the concrete, causal order are claimed to be direct implications of his embrace of discredited *verificationism*, the view that only objectively detectable properties are real (Searle 1995, p. 59). Furthermore, his claim that intentional states are not parts of the concrete causal order but, rather, abstractions that help track real patterns is deemed problematic for at least three additional reasons: (1) as we saw in chapter 6, Churchland worries that any theory known to be false has some predictive utility and, therefore, tracks a real pattern (1989, p. 126); (2) the claim risks circularity: intentionality is defined in terms of perspectives, which are, after all, intentional phenomena (Fodor and Lepore 1993, p. 76), and (3) if intentional states are nothing but abstract categories useful for tracking real patterns, then how can they be selected for in evolution: how can they make a *difference* to the reproductive success of organisms (Fodor and Lepore 1993, p. 74)?

Intentionality

Let me begin with the points about intentionality. It certainly seems correct to say that, according to the ordinary manifest concept of intentionality, intentional states have causal powers. My belief that it is raining and my desire to stay dry can combine to cause me to open my umbrella. Many philosophers conclude from this that intentional states must be more than mere abstractions useful for tracking real patterns in human behaviour. For a belief and desire to cause my limbs to go through the motions necessary to open my umbrella, they must be concrete, datable events in the brain. In other words, the causal power of intentional states implies that they must be identifiable with brain states.

But Dennett can legitimately resist this inference. The assumption that intentional states have causal powers need not imply that they have causal powers in the same sense that brain states have causal powers. Any view that accepts that intentional states can *explain* or *make sense of* behaviour arguably does justice to the ordinary notion of intentionality. And it is clear that Dennett's view acknowledges an important explanatory role for intentional states.

However, Dennett's view remains problematic for the following reason. According to an influential interpretation of the commonsense view that intentional states have causal powers (Davidson 2001, pp. 9–11; Ramsey, Stich and Garon 1995, pp. 205–6), if two or more distinct sets of intentional states are equally good explanations of some behavioural sequence, there must be a fact of the matter concerning which set did the actual causing. Consider a case discussed by Dennett: a famous art critic named Sam swears for decades that his son's mediocre art has value; he goes to his deathbed without recanting (BS 39–40). As Dennett notes, there are at least two distinct sets of intentional states that are equally good explanations of this behaviour. Either, (1) the art critic is so biased by love for his son that his judgement is impaired and he actually believes that the mediocre art has value, or (2) the art critic does not believe that the mediocre art has value, but maintains this out of loyalty to his son. Dennett argues that

> [even if we] were able to determine that Sam's last *judgment* on his deathbed was, 'My only consolation is that I fathered a great artist,' we could still hold that the issue between the warring hypotheses was undecided, for this judgement may have been a self-deception … If discovering a man's judgements still leaves the matter of belief

ascription undecided, and if in fact either ascription of belief accounts for, explains, predicts Sam's behaviour as well as the other, are we so sure that Sam determinately had one belief or the other? Are we sure there is a difference between his really and truly believing his son is a good artist, and his deceiving himself out of love while knowing the truth in his heart of hearts?

(BS, p. 49)

According to some philosophers, there must be a fact of the matter in such cases. Whether or not Sam's external behaviour betrays it, one of these two beliefs is doing the actual causing in Sam's brain. This is at odds with Dennett's view that intentional states like beliefs are merely abstract tools for tracking real patterns in behaviour. When two distinct belief ascriptions do an equally good job of tracking the real pattern, then there is no deeper fact, for instance, no mentalese sentence written in the brain, which can settle which belief ascription is really true. It is unclear to me whether this view is really at odds with our ordinary intuitions about the causal powers of intentional states. I think we often find ourselves doing things without being clear about the reasons for them; the beliefs and desires that explain them. In such cases, it seems plausible to acknowledge that there may be no answer to the question of which belief or desire really causes the behaviour. Answers are only forthcoming at a lower level that tracks the neural/physical causes of behaviour, rather than at the intentional level, from which we track possible *reasons* for behaviour. But this certainly conflicts with the intuitions of many philosophers, who claim that in such cases there must be a fact of the matter about which of two or more sets of intentional states do the real causing.

Dennett can respond to such worries in two ways. He can either push the view that the ordinary concept of intentionality allows for cases where multiple intentional explanations are equally good and there is no deeper fact of the matter. Alternatively, he can grant that this implication of his view is at odds with common sense and constitutes a revision of the ordinary concept of intentionality, so as to make it more compatible with the scientific image. The latter strategy would require showing that what we know about the brain makes it unlikely that there are neural facts that determine which of two equally explanatory though distinct beliefs actually cause some pattern of behaviour. Given the difficulty philosophers and scientists have had in identifying anything like determinate mentalese sentences in the brain, Dennett appears to be on solid ground here. However, his philosophical critics complain that his intuitions are artefacts of the verificationism and behaviourism he inherits from Ryle. This temperament leads Dennett to doubt the reality of mental distinctions that make no difference to observable behaviour. I address this general complaint below.

Besides allegedly contradicting the common-sense assumption that intentional states have causal powers, Dennett's understanding of intentionality is sometimes charged with circularity: he seems to define intentionality as a real pattern discernible from a perspective, and perspectives are intentional phenomena (Fodor and Lepore 1993, p. 76). This is not entirely fair to Dennett: he is clear that a real pattern is there whether or not it is spotted by anyone (BC, p. 102). Even so, one might complain that such patterns are too ephemeral to be 'really real'. As we saw at the end of chapter 6, Churchland complains that all sorts of false theories track real patterns in Dennett's sense, e.g., we can discern a pattern in the motion of celestial bodies from the geocentric stance, i.e., by assuming that the earth is the centre of the cosmos. In addition, as Fodor and Lepore (1993, p. 74) note, if intentional states are not concrete, causally implicated features of the world but, rather, mere abstractions that enable us to track higher-level patterns, then it is hard to see how they can make a difference to our survival and, therefore, how they can be selected for in evolution.

I think that Dennett's view has the resources to defuse such worries. The real pattern discernible from the intentional stance is grounded in an objectively real, concrete, physical phenomenon: replicators. There are physico-chemical structures that persist in the face of entropy, nature's inevitable trend towards dissolution, by making as many copies of themselves as possible. Because such copying requires resources, such resources are limited and many different kinds of replicators compete for these limited resources, those that are better at acquiring resources will replicate more than those that are worse at acquiring resources. This is natural selection, and it is as concrete and real as any other physical process. However, this process and the behaviour of its products are extremely difficult to track using the concepts of the physical sciences alone. And there are good physical reasons for this. Such selection processes are extremely sensitive to minor variations in environmental conditions. A slight mutation may immediately die out in one environment, or quickly come to dominate a population in an environment that differs only slightly along some physical dimension. It is physically impossible to measure with sufficient accuracy every physical variable that is potentially relevant to determining the course of natural selection. So, as Dennett puts it, the inapplicability of the physical stance to such physical phenomena is not merely a 'parochial' limitation on human science. No physically possible science could track phenomena like natural selection or the behaviour of its products from the physical stance (ER, pp. 151–152).

For this reason, natural selection and its products must be tracked from higher-level stances, like the design stance and the intentional stance. Although most concrete, physical causes implicated in such phenomena are invisible from such stances, *significant* ones 'pop out'. Where natural selection operates, we can expect the prevalence of replicators that are *good* at acquiring resources necessary for replication relative to an environment. This justifies focusing just on those variables that are relevant to successful replication, or, in other words, assuming the intentional stance towards replicators. We are lucky enough to have the capacity for assuming the intentional stance towards such systems, which are not trackable from the physical stance, because we ourselves are replicators selected for our abilities to compete for scarce resources. Among these is the ability to track our fellow replicators from the intentional stance.

This picture offers a response to scepticism concerning Dennett's 'mild realism' about intentionality (BC, p. 98). Contrary to Churchland's suggestion, the real pattern tracked from the intentional stance is more robust than the real pattern tracked by false theories like geocentric astronomy. While the perspective on celestial bodies that human beings have from the surface of the earth is indeed parochial, the perspective that we must adopt towards products of natural selection is not. Churchland himself argues that natural selection and its products constitute a natural kind with important physical properties in common: they are non-equilibrium thermodynamic systems (1982, p. 233). As I explained above, these are precisely the sorts of systems that are notoriously sensitive to environmental conditions, in a way that makes them impossible to track from the physical stance. Thus, the *physical* properties of such systems *explain why* they require explanation in other terms, e.g., the design stance and the intentional stance. So the real patterns discernible from the intentional stance are grounded in a concrete, physically robust, perspective-independent phenomenon.

This also suggests a response to Fodor and Lepore's worry. Although intentional states are not concrete events that can affect natural selection, natural selection is guaranteed to give rise to systems the behaviour of which can only be tracked by ascribing goals and access to information. There are principled physical reasons for this. So Fodor and Lepore's criticism is off the mark. Although natural selection does not, strictly speaking, select for intentional states, it selects for mechanisms and dispositions to behaviour that can only be tracked via the ascription of intentional states. And this is a pattern that any complete description of the universe must acknowledge.

To sum up: for Dennett, intentional *systems* are objectively real, concrete members of the causal order. These are systems that are products of natural selection and, therefore, sensitive to environmental conditions to a degree that makes them impossible to track from the physical stance. We are examples of such systems, and we have developed tools for tracking our own kind: the design stance and the intentional stance. Though the *states* we ascribe from these stances are abstract, the systems to which they apply and the behaviour they enable us to track are as real and significant as any other natural phenomenon.

Qualia

As we saw in chapter 3, to most philosophers, by far the most outrageous component of Dennett's system is his scepticism about qualia. What can be more obvious than the redness of red, the painfulness of pain, the taste of red wine, etc.? Yet many read Dennett as *denying* that such properties exist. Any 'explanation' of consciousness that leaves these properties out, according to such critics, throws the baby out with the bathwater (Strawson 1992; Block 1993; Searle 1995). Dennett often argues that qualia, as many philosophers implicitly understand them, do not exist (Dennett 1988; CE, pp. 365–6, 372, 459–60; SD, p. 177). He even quips that, given the way philosophers define 'zombies', as creatures indistinguishable from us except for lacking qualia, we are all zombies (CE, p. 406). But these are just rhetorical flourishes. Anyone who claims that Dennett denies that the redness of red, the painfulness of pain, the taste of red wine, etc., are real phenomena seriously misrepresents his view.

Dennett argues that the term 'qualia,' as most philosophers use it, is a term of art, the use of which implicitly endorses a theory that Dennett thinks is false: the theory that the mind is a Cartesian Theatre, i.e., a non-physical place filled with appearances that make no difference of any kind detectable from the third person. If qualia are supposed to be, by definition, intrinsic, ineffable and subjective, then they can make no objectively detectable difference by *definition.* To countenance the existence of such phenomena is, according to Dennett, to rule out the relevance of science by fiat (CE, p. 403). For this reason, if qualia are defined in this way, they are incompatible with Dennett's guiding assumption that standard science tells us everything there is to know about what exists. As a consequence, he concludes that qualia, so defined, do not exist.

But this is not the same as denying the existence of phenomena that many philosophers *call* qualia. The redness of red, the painfulness of pain, the taste of wine, etc., all exist according to Dennett. They just are not qualia, as philosophers understand this term. For example, as we saw in chapter 4, for Dennett, colour is a reflectance property of surfaces of objects. This property only seems ineffable because it is hard to express in words. Sensory systems have co-evolved with such properties over eons such that they are tailor-made for each other, like two halves of a torn Jell-o box. The only practical means for efficiently detecting colours is using the sensory apparatus that has co-evolved with colours for this purpose. The richness of the contents of conscious experience consists, according to Dennett, in the richness of the *external* properties that we represent in conscious experience (CE, p. 408). Our beloved qualia are not intrinsic, non-physical, ineffable, subjective properties of our brains; rather, if they are anything, they are perfectly objective, physical properties of our environment, which are practically impossible to express using words.

So, Dennett is not an *eliminativist* about the kinds of properties that are often called qualia. If anything, he is a *representationalist*: he believes the things philosophers call qualia are, typically, environmental properties *represented* by experiential brain states (CE, pp. 372–3). This theory may be false, but to claim that Dennett denies the existence of the obvious is to seriously misrepresent his view: it is to attack a 'straw man'.

Verificationism

The dramatic differences between Dennett and many of his philosophical antagonists are often traced, by both sides, to a fundamental methodological/metaphysical assumption. Dennett is accused of, and acknowledges, with some qualifications, allegiance to *verificationism*. This view can be summarized with the following slogan: the only real difference is an objectively detectable difference. The reason Dennett is sceptical about qualia, as philosophers understand them, and consequently, about the possibility of zombies, is because qualia are *defined* such that they can make absolutely no objectively detectable difference. If they made a difference, then we could tell whether someone is a zombie or not. The reason that Dennett doubts that there is some further deeper fact, beyond patterns of observable behaviour, that fixes what an agent really believes, is because he cannot see how such a fact could make an objectively detectable difference. If it made a difference, then we could notice it in observable behaviour.

Verificationism has been out of favour with philosophers since its heyday in the mid-twentieth century. Classical forms of verificationism have deep problems. In essence, verificationism is the view that something is real only if there is some means of testing for it, some form of potential evidence for it. Classical verificationism assumes very restricted notions of testing and evidence. On one view, for example, distinctions are real only if they can make a difference to our sensory experiences. Philosophical or logical behaviourism is a form of classical verificationism: it holds that mental states are real only to the degree that they make a difference to publicly observable behaviour. Such forms of verificationism are clearly too restrictive to be plausible. As the history of science has shown, we cannot know in advance what forms evidence confirming the existence of some distinction will take.

However, Dennett's verificationism is more subtle and minimal. He calls it 'urbane verificationism' (CE, p. 461). It is more of a methodological wariness than a positive program. All that Dennett claims is that we should be wary of concepts the veridicality of which is, *by definition*, untestable. He does not deny that many hypotheses may not be testable by current scientific methods, or that we might not be able today to imagine what difference some distinction might make. However, concepts that are defined so as to preclude any means of intersubjective testing are, on Dennett's view, suspect. And his most controversial claims reflect this temperament. He is sceptical of qualia, as philosophers understand them, because they are defined as objectively undetectable, *in principle*. He doubts the possibility of zombies, because these creatures are supposed to be, in principle, objectively indistinguishable from conscious persons. For the same reason he doubts distinctions among beliefs that make no conceivable difference to observable behaviour.

I think it is hard to quarrel with Dennett's urbane verificationism. It is not doctrinaire in the least. It simply shifts the burden of proof in the appropriate direction. If no conceivable scientific evidence can pick between two hypotheses, then we are justified in presuming that there is no real distinction between them, *until* someone discovers evidence that does pick between them. If this is Dennett's attitude, then his scepticism about qualia and other currently verification-transcendent mental phenomena is merely tentative. He is not ruling out the possibility that such phenomena exist;

rather, he is merely shifting the burden of proof: if he is to accept that they exist, then he must be shown what difference their existence makes.[2] Of course, Dennett's antagonists insist that qualia and their ilk do make detectable differences; however, these differences are only detectable from the subjective, first person perspective. But Dennett is sceptical of such objectively undetectable, subjective differences (CE, pp. 126, 403–4). He prefers to attribute such intuitions to misguided theorizing (CE, p. 461).

Final words

As promised in chapter 1, the preceding has been a whirlwind tour. Much ground has been covered, often not as thoroughly as it deserves. Dennett's thought is extremely rich and wide-ranging, and no introduction of this size can hope to do justice to all of it. I hope I have at least whetted the reader's appetite for further exploration of Dennett's corpus and the enormous literature that it has generated. In these final pages, I want to provide a very slight taste of important issues I have regrettably been forced to ignore, and suggest two important areas of Dennett's thought that I think require further development.

The greatest lacuna in the foregoing is the dearth of discussion of Dennett's engagement with non-philosophers. In chapter 5, I briefly discussed his criticisms of Libet's conclusions about the inefficacy of conscious will; however, Dennett's contributions to the scientific study of consciousness are far more substantial than my discussion suggests. Large portions of *Consciousness Explained* (1991) are devoted to detailed discussions of experiments in the cognitive neuroscience of conscious perception. Dennett's proposals have been engaged by numerous cognitive neuroscientists. A good source for such exchanges is the discussion article he published with the psychologist Marcel Kinsbourne (Dennett and Kinsbourne 1992), from which much of the material in *Consciousness Explained* is drawn. Churchland and Ramachandran's (1993) criticism of Dennett's theory of conscious visual perception and his response are another good example of his engagement with cognitive neuroscience.

Earlier in his career, and more recently as well, Dennett has similarly engaged researchers in artificial intelligence. Many of his favourite intuition pumps are drawn from actual research programs in AI. He was one of the first philosophers to appreciate the philosophical importance of AI research, as is evident in the 1978 article, 'Artificial intelligence as philosophy and psychology' (BS, pp. 109–26). His discussion of the 'frame problem' (BC, pp. 181–205) is a classic exposition and exploration of a deeply philosophical problem that, at first, seemed to many a mere technical problem in AI. And, in the mid- to late-1990s Dennett was an active participant in Rodney Brooks' attempt to build a humanoid robot known as 'Cog' (BC, pp. 153–70), in the MIT AI lab.

Dennett's contributions to cognitive ethology and developmental psychology are also noteworthy. He is one of the first proponents of the standard psychological test for higher-order thought in non-human animals and children: the false belief task. He argues that a subject's grasp of deception is a good indicator of whether they can have thoughts about other thoughts. In order to deceive, a subject must assume that the object of their deception represents the world differently than it is, and this requires a capacity to think about another's thoughts, i.e., to have higher-order thoughts. The proposal is already present in his early paper, 'Conditions of personhood' (BS 275). Dennett explores it in much greater depth in the discussion article, 'Intentional systems in Cognitive ethology: the "Panglossian Paradigm" defended' (1983; IS, pp. 237–68). The original version contains discussion of his proposals by cognitive ethologists. The reprinted version includes a supplement, 'Reflections: interpreting monkeys, theorists, and genes' (IS, pp. 269–86), which updates his views in the light of experiences in the field with cognitive ethologists studying vervet monkeys in Africa.

As a philosopher, I have naturally focused on Dennett's contributions to philosophy and exchanges with philosophers. However, anyone interested in the cognitive sciences will be richly rewarded by exploring Dennett's engagement with, and influence on non-philosophers.

Let me conclude by returning to philosophy, and registering two respects in which, I think, Dennett's system could use further

philosophical development. The first concerns the nature of normativity. As we have seen, normative assumptions are central to many
of Dennett's proposals. At the most basic level, both the design and
the intentional stances make normative assumptions: they assume
that systems will behave as they *should*. The ascription of intentional states, for Dennett, presupposes that the object of ascription
approximates norms of rationality. As we saw in chapter 5, Dennett
also stresses the role that efficacious communal norms play in the
evolution of human freedom. In *Freedom Evolves* (2003), he
addresses the problem of normativity explicitly. He proposes that we
can somehow bootstrap from the historically contingent norms that
have governed human societies 'all the way to norms that command
assent in all rational agents' (FE, p. 303). He compares this to the historical process whereby human beings learned to draw increasingly
straight lines, thereby approximating 'the eternal Platonic Form of
the Straight' (FE, p. 303). But this discussion appears to conflate
bootstrapping increasingly accurate *approximations* of norms, with
bootstrapping the *discovery* of norms and normativity.

Dennett's corpus is filled with plausible speculations about how
systems that better *approximate* certain normative standards might
evolve from systems that are poorer approximations of such standards, but nowhere does he give a satisfactory account of where the
very concept of normativity comes from. Human beings are not just
good approximations to rational norms. They understand the distinction between norms and approximations to them, and are able
to apply such distinctions, for example, when explaining systems
from the intentional stance. But this is puzzling. How can a system
that has always merely approximated norms ever develop the concept of a norm? To use Dennett's analogy, we could never gauge our
progress at drawing a straight line without first appreciating the
appropriate norm, what Dennett flippantly calls 'the eternal Platonic Form of the Straight.' But how did we ever come up with such
an idea in the first place, and how did we ever come up with the
rational norms that govern the intentional stance?

Dennett's published work does not contain a worked-out solution to this problem. Yet it is one of the oldest and deepest puzzles
about the mind. It leads Plato to the conclusion that, prior to our

earthly lives, we lived among the Forms, and our knowledge of them in this life is mere recollection of that past life. It leads Descartes to the conclusion that a perfect, limitless being (God) put the idea of perfection in our minds. These 'solutions' are non-starters for naturalists like Dennett. But the problem that drives Plato and Descartes to such desperate lengths is just as pressing for Dennett. If we succeed only in approximating norms, and if we are exposed only to approximations of norms, then how do we ever acquire the idea of normativity?

A second respect in which Dennett's system could use further development concerns a certain self-referential dynamic that I think he has largely ignored in his published work. This problem arises most clearly for his theory of consciousness. According to Dennett, the Cartesian Theatre is an illusion that nonetheless persists because of the important role it plays in organizing information flow in the brain. In his terms, it is a meme-complex that does not track anything real in the brain, but nonetheless earns its keep thanks to its practical effects: it helps us solve the higher order problem of cognitive control. It is important to remember, however, that Dennett is urging a *replacement* of the Cartesian Theatre meme-complex with a *different* meme-complex, the 'fame in the brain' meme-complex. And his grounds for urging this are purely epistemic: the fame in the brain meme-complex is a more *accurate* representation of the workings of the mind than the Cartesian Theatre meme-complex. But this raises a question: since the Cartesian Theatre meme-complex has largely earned its keep because of its practical effects on neural processing, and not because of its veridicality, is it rational to replace it with an alternative which, though possibly veridical, is not tested in this practical role?

A brain that thinks of itself as a Cartesian Theatre potentially engages in very different strategies of cognitive control than a brain that thinks of itself in terms of fame in the brain. To *truly* believe that one's mind is a Cartesian Theatre is very different from believing that the Cartesian Theatre is merely a useful user illusion. It is possible that this difference has no effects on how brains control information flow. Nevertheless, Dennett's view has implications for itself that must be acknowledged. The fame in the brain model is just another meme-complex, and the brains that it parasitizes will thereby cease to be parasitized by the Cartesian Theatre meme-complex. But, if the Cartesian Theatre plays such an important role in controlling information flow, Dennett's advocacy of his alternative carries risks. On Dennett's own view, it is possible that replacing the Cartesian Theatre with fame in the brain significantly changes the nature of human consciousness, for good or ill. It is rather like upgrading the operating system on one's computer.

This is a variation on a general theme that Dennett acknowledges in places, particularly in *Freedom Evolves* (pp. 14, 16–21, 305). Any theory that replaces traditional manifest concepts with more veridical surrogates, must explain why the traditional versions persisted despite being misleading. Such explanations invariably appeal to their utility: it is useful to think of ourselves as free, rational, conscious agents, in the traditional sense. But then, when these concepts are replaced with more veridical surrogates, there is always a risk that the pragmatic functions that the originals performed will be compromised. Dennett often points out that we are 'creatures of our own attempts to make sense of ourselves' (IS, p. 91).[3] And he notes the important roles that traditional self-conceptions play in our cognitive lives. Yet at the same time, he wants to replace these self-conceptions with updated versions, and it is unclear whether these updated versions can play all the same important roles.

This issue has implications for the persistence of anti-scientific self-conceptions in the modern world. For Dennett's views to really take hold, by his own lights, they must be more than true. They must win the competition with other memes for control of human brains. But, as Dennett often points out, the robustness of a meme is no indication of its truth (CE, pp. 205–6). It is possible that anti-scientific memes are so useful to most human brains that they are very hard to dislodge. In fact, it is possible that anti-scientific memes are *better* at controlling information flow in many brains than science-friendly surrogates such as those proposed by Dennett. This might explain the animosity that his views encounter. An appreciation of how his system applies to itself should lead Dennett and his admirers to further explore such issues.

Indeed, Dennett seems to have turned his attention to issues in this vicinity. His most recent book, *Breaking the Spell: Religion as a Natural Phenomenon* (2006), articulates a detailed, scientific approach to the study of religion and its role in human life. He argues that religion is a *memetic* phenomenon: it is an artefact of memes to which human brains are particularly prone. Among these is the meme for sacrilege: the prohibition on questioning religious belief. This explains, for Dennett, much of the resistance that scientific scepticism encounters. Dennett's intellectual odyssey is far from over.

Notes

Preface

1. For a good discussion of this, see Ross 2000, pp. 13–19. For good examples of this, see Dennett 2000.
2. I recommend his published discussion of this question (Ross 2000, especially pp. 13–25).

Chapter one

1. To be fair, none of these theorists rejects all parts of the manifest image. In fact, over the course of his career, Stich has retreated from his early scepticism regarding the manifest concept of belief.
2. At least not homunculi as smart as whole persons. More on this in chapter 2.
3. Dualists have sophisticated responses to these sorts of objections. However, it remains controversial whether these responses work.
4. Eliminativists have sophisticated responses to this sort of objection. However, it remains controversial whether these responses work.
5. By this, I mean that different kinds of brains, like different kinds of computers, can execute the same functions.

Chapter two

1. Or desirers, or hopers, etc. From now on, for ease of exposition, I refer to propositional attitudes in general as

'beliefs' and systems containing propositional attitudes in general as 'believers', but everything I say applies equally to other kinds of propositional attitudes.

2. For example, a chess-playing program may include a command to move the Queen out early. In cases where this is not the optimal move, the intentional stance will fail to predict the program's behaviour.

3. There is a tradition in philosophy of mind and language, of which Dennett is a part, that sees such charitable assumptions of rationality as a central constraint on interpreting what others are saying or thinking (see Quine 1960, p. 219; Davidson 1984, pp. 136–7, 152–3).

4. See especially Marr 1982.

5. For example, luminance contrast detectors and other specialized processors of visual information.

6. For example, if it turns out that the brain is not running a 'mentalese' programming language.

7. At least as Dennett understood him at the time.

8. That is the point of the often humorous contrast between the human characters on the television series *Star Trek*, and the ultra-logical, alien Mr. Spock.

9. Here I draw on Dennett's own discussion (IS, p. 25) of an objection originally raised by the philosopher Robert Nozick.

10. This point counts equally for some behaviours of non-human animals, and some computers.

11. I shall have much more to say about Dennett's notion of a real pattern, and whether it helps him avoid the charge of instrumentalism, in chapters 6 and 7.

Chapter three

1. As I explain in chapter 4, this does not mean that, for Dennett, there is no self. Dennett argues that the self can be real even if it is not, strictly speaking, located in the brain.

2. Ryle (1949), Wittgenstein (1953), Sellars (1956) and Quine (1960) are probably the most influential sources of this tradition.

3. Many philosophers agree with Dennett that the Cartesian Theatre cannot be 'housed' within the nervous system: its properties cannot be explained by the activity of the nervous system. However, unlike Dennett, many do not conclude that the doctrine of the Cartesian Theatre must be abandoned. Rather, they conclude that science

cannot explain consciousness. See especially Nagel (1974), Jackson (1982), Levine (1983), Chalmers (1996) and McGinn (1999).

4. When philosophers use the word 'intuition', they mean something like 'unreflective, gut reaction'. Given some puzzle or question, we can ask people which proposed solution or answer they are initially inclined to accept, without thinking too hard about it. Philosophers call such queries 'appeals to intuition', and such solutions or answers 'intuitive'.

5. As Dennett quips, 'some of your best friends might be zombies!' (CE, p. 73).

6. Including her body and clothing, which have been painted black and white, and any monitor used to convey data.

7. This was also the methodology of an early school of psychology known as *Introspectionism* (Titchener 1898, p. 27).

8. Dennett often complains about the 'visual' understanding of intro-spection: literally, the word 'introspection' means something like 'inner-looking'. The implication is that when we introspect, we *observe* exactly what is in consciousness; there is no theorizing involved. Dennett argues that introspection is better viewed as a kind of 'impromptu theorizing' (CE, p. 67) about one's own mind – theorizing that is unconstrained by public verification.

9. For an explicit discussion of the distinction between interpretation constrained by the rationality assumption and interpretation constrained by the assumption of first-person authority, see BS, pp. 19–21.

10. It is not clear that this is true of typical subjects in every culture. Remember Dennett's suggestion that introspection is 'impromptu theorizing' rather than direct observation of the facts of conscious-ness. If different cultures assume different theories about the nature of the mind, then we might expect cultural differences in subjects' judge-ments about their minds, and consequently, cultural differences in their heterophenomenological worlds. The Cartesian Theatre may be a peculiarly Western way for a subject to conceive of their mind.

11. Indeed, some conspiracy theorists believe this.

12. Dennett often employs a similar sociopolitical metaphor when explaining his theory (SD, pp. 133, 137, 141).

13. This has important implications for Dennett's view on the conscious-ness of non-human animals. I explore these in detail in chapter 4.

14. If they did, then we would be able to tell conscious persons apart from their zombie duplicates, just by interviewing them.

Chapter four

1. These operations are actions that 'stupid' homunculi, in Dennett's sense, can execute: scanning, printing and erasing symbols for the most part. In digital computers, this amounts to altering strings of 1s and 0s, or, in other words, flipping switches between 'on' (1) and 'off' (0).

2. The series of steps children are taught to do long division is an example of an algorithm.

3. In fact, according to Dennett (CE, p. 212), the Turing Machine architecture, and by extension, the von Neumann machine architecture, were inspired by Turing's introspection of his own highly rational stream of consciousness: he solved problems by first decomposing them into a series of steps and then bringing simple operations to bear on relevant information in sequence.

4. After Kipling's (1912) collection of fanciful stories about the origins of animal traits. I say more about this complaint in chapter 6, where I discuss Dennett's defence of Darwinism in evolutionary biology.

5. Since replicators have reasons to do things, based on their goals (surviving and replicating), they count as *intentional systems*: we can predict their behaviour by assuming that they pursue their goals in the most rational way possible, given the information to which they have access. Given Dennett's claim that all it takes to be a believer is to be an intentional system (see chapter 2), this means that replicators count as very rudimentary believers. The reasons for which such rudimentary believers do things need not be recognized by anyone. In Dennett's terms, they are 'free-floating rationales' (IS 259). This concept is important to understanding the connections between the intentional stance and Darwin's theory of natural selection. I discuss free-floating rationales in more detail in chapter 6, where I treat Dennett's defence of the Darwinian understanding of evolution.

6. As Dennett and many others have remarked, this can be compared to the process of getting tenure in the academic world (CE, p. 177).

7. All human beings, no matter how intelligent and creative, 'stand on the shoulders of giants'. Beethoven could not have composed his symphonies starting from scratch, that is, without first acquiring his musical knowledge from others, who passed on a rich cultural heritage accumulated over hundreds of generations.

8. Dennett's latest book, *Breaking the Spell: Religion as a Natural Phenomenon* (2006), proposes this memetic model as part of a scientific explanation of religious belief.

9. I thank James Petrik for this excellent example of a pernicious meme.

10. I shall have more to say about this kind of realism in chapter 6, where I discuss Dennett's theory of real patterns.

11. There are many other problems that have been raised for Dennett's theory, some by philosophers, and some by scientists. I briefly review some of these in the concluding chapter of the book.

12. What I say here holds equally for other sensory systems and the properties they detect.

13. See Tittle (2005) for an amazingly thorough and concise compendium of scores of classic, philosophical thought experiments.

14. This is analogous to the distinction, discussed in chapter 2, between what *makes* something an intentional system, and hence, for Dennett, a believer, and what *causes* something to achieve this status.

Chapter five

1. This is distinct from the political doctrine of the same name.

2. Dennett's notion of an intentional system, a surrogate for the ordinary concept of a believer, applies to thermostats, and his method of heterophenomenology and theory of the conscious self do comparable violence to the ordinary concepts from which they derive.

3. More on this in chapter 6.

4. The nineteenth-century French physicist Laplace articulated the deterministic assumptions of Newtonian physics in terms of an imaginary demon that could determine, with perfect precision, the position and momentum of every particle in the universe at some time, t. Given Newton's laws, and the demon's supposedly unlimited computational powers, the demon could compute the precise state of the universe at any time before or after t.

5. For example genetic factors or early childhood experiences.

6. For example, the batting averages of all minor league players whose middle names begin with 'N' sampled every thirteen days.

7. This is an example of one of Dennett's favourite and most controversial argumentative strategies: Show that a difference posited on philosophical grounds makes no *detectable* difference, and then argue that it is not a real difference. If, like qualia, genuinely random self-forming actions make no detectable difference, to the agent or observers, then why posit them? Such arguments provoke

dismissive responses because, as Dennett admits, they appeal to a kind of *verificationism*: real differences must be *detectable*, at least in principle. I discuss this feature of Dennett's views at greater length in the concluding chapter.

8. Dennett first uses this slogan in *Elbow Room* (1984), and in *Freedom Evolves* (2003), he calls this 'probably the most important sentence' (p. 122n) in that earlier book.

9. That is, in Dennett's terms, any animal that counts as a 'Popperian creature' (BS, p. 77; DDI, pp. 375–7; FE, p. 248).

10. Here Dennett draws heavily on recent proposals of the psychiatrist George Ainslie (2001).

11. Even if the long-term pay-off of not yielding exceeds the short-term pay-off of yielding.

12. This example is drawn from Dennett's discussion (FE, pp. 207–12) of Ainslie (2001).

Chapter six

1. Given Dennett's understanding of his own view as a complex of memes competing for survival and reproduction, this characterization of Dennett's reconceptualizations is more than a metaphor. I explore this in more detail in the concluding chapter.

2. See, for example, CE, pp. 231–41.

3. The emergence of new species.

4. Dennett points out that this analogy is actually ill-chosen. There are other ways of mounting a dome on rounded arches, but these are much less beautiful than pendentives. In fact, pendentives are close to optimal solutions to problems that likely faced San Marco's designers: they occupy close to the minimal surface area required to support the dome, and contain a smooth surface ideal for mounting mosaics. As Dennett puts it, 'the spandrels of San Marco aren't spandrels even in Gould's extended sense. They are adaptations, chosen from a set of equipossible alternatives for largely aesthetic reasons' (DDI, p. 274).

5. This is a term from computer science for a string of units of information, or ones and zeros.

6. A good web site is http://www.bitstorm.org/gameoflife/.

7. Dennett provides excellent, detailed introductions to the game in at least four places: IS 38–38, BC, pp. 105–10, DDI, pp. 166–76, FE, pp. 36–41.

8. A Google Internet search on the word string 'game of life' yields dozens of web pages devoted to exploring, in detail, the diverse properties of the varied exotica that inhabit the Game of Life world.

Chapter seven

1. The reductionist rhetoric regarding consciousness concerns its relation to intentionality: from his earliest writings Dennett has been committed to explaining consciousness in terms of intentionality. But since, for Dennett, intentionality is itself irreducible to mechanical properties, consciousness, as an intentional phenomenon, remains irreducible to mechanical properties.
2. As a matter of fact, Dennett probably thinks that, in the case of qualia, this will never happen, because the concept is deliberately defined in such a way that it can make no objectively detectable difference.
3. See CE, p. 24 and FE, p. 305 for related discussion.

Glossary

Adaptationism   The view of most evolutionary biologists that the prevalence of traits in populations of organisms can be explained by the fact that they are adaptive, i.e., useful to survival and reproduction.

Agency   The property of being an agent, that is, a system the behaviour of which can be explained as the outcome of deliberation about how best to achieve goals in the light of information.

Cartesian Theatre   Dennett's term for a traditional, philosophical model of the conscious mind that he rejects. According to this model, derived from Descartes, the conscious mind is like a theatre in which the self observes appearances.

Category mistake   Gilbert Ryle's term for the misapplication of a concept to an inappropriate domain. For example, Dennett thinks that applying the distinction between observed and yet-to-be-observed within the brain is a category mistake.

Centre of narrative gravity   Dennett's model of the conscious self. It is the fictional 'narrator' we must hypothesize as the source of the narratives that brains construct in order to control information flow.

Co-evolution   Biological phenomenon in which multiple traits act as selection pressures on each other, causing dramatic amplifications of evolution. Dennett argues that the colours of edible plants co-evolved with the capacity to discriminate colours.

Compatibilism Philosophical position on the problem of freedom of the will, according to which behaviour can be entirely determined and freely chosen at the same time: determinism and freedom of the will are compatible.

Consciousness What it is like to be a sentient creature. According to the philosophical tradition, conscious states are accessible only to the subject undergoing them, and are ineffable, or impossible to fully express in public language.

Crane Dennett's term for any variant on Darwin's mechanism of natural selection used to explain the evolution of design in nature. In contrast to skyhooks, cranes are legitimate evolutionary explanations grounded in non-mysterious, mechanical processes.

Darwinism The view that all examples of intelligence and design in nature succumb to explanations of the kind introduced by Darwin, in his theory of evolution by natural selection.

Derived intentionality A representation has derived intentionality if it inherits its status as a representation from some other representational system. For example, the word 'cat' stands for cats, but this status is derived from the intentions of human language users.

Design space The space of all possible designed objects, from amoebas, to Ford Model Ts, to Einstein's Theory of Relativity. Dennett thinks of natural selection and its variants as algorithms for exploring this immense space.

Design stance A framework, first made explicit by Dennett, for explaining and predicting systems based on the assumption that they will behave as designed, for example, predicting that one's alarm clock will ring based on the fact that it is designed to ring when you want it to ring.

Dualism The view that human beings are composed of two fundamentally different kinds of substances: physical and mental, or that human beings have two fundamentally different kinds of properties: physical and mental.

Eliminativism The view that some putative object or property should be eliminated from our worldview. For example, most people are eliminativists about witches. Some contemporary philosophers have argued for eliminativism about mental states like beliefs.

Epistemic   Having to do with what can be known, as opposed to what is the case. So, for example, an epistemic possibility is something that is possible for all we can know, as opposed to something that is *truly* possible.

Essentialism   The view that objects, properties, states and events have essences, i.e., properties that are necessary to belong to some kind. For example, an essentialist might claim that an animal cannot be a mammal unless its parents are mammals.

Exaptation   Stephen Jay Gould's term for a biological trait the function of which is not the function for which it was selected in evolution.

Extended phenotype   Richard Dawkins' term for objects and structures which are not parts of an organism's body, yet which the organism's genes 'assume' are present for integration into crucial biological functions, for example the spider's web.

Fame in the brain   Dennett's model of the conscious mind – an alternative to the Cartesian Theatre. Consciousness consists of the motley sequence of neurocomputational agents that happen to achieve disproportionate influence on the brain's long-term, overall activity.

Folk psychology   Our common-sense understanding of 'what makes people tick'. According to philosophical tradition, this involves explaining human behaviour in terms of beliefs, desires, sensations, and other mental states.

Freedom of the will   To say that human beings have freedom of the will is to say that we have the power to freely choose some of our actions, i.e., that some decisions are entirely up to us, and cannot be blamed on factors beyond our control.

Free-floating rationale   Dennett's term for a reason to do something that is not represented by any mind. For example, plants have reasons to grow leaves, but before human beings started studying plants, no one *knew* what these reasons were.

Functionalism   A philosophical theory about the relationship between the mind and the brain. The mind is identical to certain functions of the brain, e.g., thought, desire, memory, perception, etc. In one version, the mind is like a computer program, running on the 'wetware' of the brain.

Gradualism   The Darwinian thesis that evolution and speciation are the result of the gradual accumulation of incremental adaptations.

Hard determinism   A philosophical position on the problem of freedom of the will, according to which freedom of the will is an illusion. All of our behaviour, even that which appears to be freely chosen, is actually the result of factors beyond our control, like genetic endowment.

Heterophenomenology   Dennett's objective, scientific method for studying consciousness. The theorist constructs a subject's 'heterophenomenological world' based on transcripts of her utterances about her conscious experiences.

Homunculus problem   This problem arises for explanations of intelligence in cognitive science. Any explanation that appeals, either overtly or covertly, to an agent within the mind, that is just as intelligent as the agent being explained, encounters this problem.

Incompatibilism   Philosophical position on the problem of freedom of the will, according to which freedom of the will and determinism are incompatible: it is impossible for a behaviour to be entirely determined and freely chosen at the same time. Hard determinism and libertarianism are varieties of incompatibilism.

Indeterminism   Philosophical position on the problem of freedom of the will, according to which some decisions are completely undetermined by preceding causal factors, and therefore, potentially free.

Ineffability   Alleged property of conscious states. A state is ineffable if it cannot be expressed in words. For example, imagine expressing to a congenitally blind person what it is like to see red.

Instrumentalism   The view that some concept or category is merely a useful tool for prediction, and does not correspond to anything real. Dennett's view that the ascription of mental states helps us track real patterns is often criticized as a kind of instrumentalism about the mind.

Intentional stance   A framework, first made explicit by Dennett, for explaining and predicting the behaviour of systems based on the assumption that they are optimally designed, or rational. One ascribes beliefs and desires the system should have and predicts it will behave in the most rational way given those beliefs and desires.

Intentionality   Property, shared by pictures, words, mental states and computational states, of standing for, being about, or representing some object, event, state, or property. For example, the word 'cat' has intentionality because it stands for cats.

Interpretationism   The view that mental states are not really real, i.e., nothing over and above what someone interprets them to be. It is closely related to instrumentalism. Dennett is often charged with advocating a kind of interpretationism.

Intrinsic   A property is intrinsic to an object if the object would have it even if there were no other objects in the world. For example, being a mother is *not* an intrinsic property. Though it is hard to think of uncontroversial examples of intrinsic properties, many philosophers take consciousness to be an intrinsic property of some mental states.

Intuition pump   Dennett's term for a thought experiment aimed at provoking intuitive reactions concerning some philosophical question. For example, suppose someone learned everything science could teach about the brain in an entirely black and white environment. If they were then shown colours, would they learn something new? Many have the intuition that yes they would.

Joycean machine   Dennett's literary/computational metaphor for the conscious mind. The stream of consciousness is like a virtual serial machine installed through the use of natural language on the parallel hardware of the brain. Dennett calls this virtual machine 'Joycean' in honour of James Joyce's stream-of-consciousness prose.

Language of thought/mentalese   The hypothesis, forcefully defended by Jerry Fodor, that human thought consists in computation conducted in a language of thought similar to a computer-programming language. Propositional attitudes are identified with sentences of the language of thought playing different roles.

Laplace's demon   Hypothetical intelligence fabricated by the French physicist Pierre-Simon Laplace to articulate the deterministic implications of Newtonian Physics. Laplace argued that if his demon were to measure the position and momentum of every physical particle in the universe at any time, it could predict the entire future and retrodict the entire history of the universe.

Libertarianism   A philosophical position on the problem of freedom of the will, according to which some human behaviour is the result of free choice and, *for this reason*, undetermined by factors beyond our control.

Logical/philosophical behaviourism   A philosophical proposal concerning the analysis of our ordinary language for talking about mental phenomena. According to logical behaviourism, words like 'pain', 'belief', 'desire', etc., must be analysed in terms of dispositions to publicly observable behaviour, rather than as referring to unobservable states of the mind.

Meme   Richard Dawkins' term for a unit of cultural selection. Just as genes are transmitted and selected for in biological evolution, memes, such as ideas, inventions, ideologies, etc., are transmitted and selected for in cultural evolution.

Mind–brain identity theory   A philosophical theory about the relationship between mind and brain. The mind is the same thing as the brain, just as water is the same thing as a substance composed of H_2O molecules.

Normativity   A phenomenon involving the distinction between correct and incorrect states or events. To judge a behaviour as irrational is to make a normative judgement. Dennett's intentional stance appeals to normative judgements about the rationality of patterns of behaviour.

Notional world   Interpretation of a system from the intentional stance enables the construction of the agent's notional world, i.e., the world as the agent takes it to be. This may not correspond to the way the world actually is. For example, the agent may believe that 'notional objects' exist, given the available evidence; just as many little children believe Santa exists.

Objective   Imagine the 'God's Eye' view of the universe, which encompasses all the facts and objects that truly exist, and only the facts and objects that truly exist. This is the objective world. It contrasts with the subjective worlds of particular, limited perspectives, which consist of the ways the world appears to those perspectives.

Original intentionality   Dennett's term for a concept that many philosophers assume only applies to human mental states. A state has original intentionality if its status as a representation derives from nothing outside of itself. According to some, words and other artefacts derive their intentionality from the intentions of human beings, which have original intentionality.

Parallel processing   A kind of computation typical of brains and connectionist computational models. It involves many simple processors processing information simultaneously, rather than one powerful processor processing information serially, i.e., one item at a time.

Phenomenology   A philosophical term for the study of phenomena, or, the way things appear. Husserl was a seminal figure in the history of phenomenology. He proposed a method for studying appearances in themselves, bracketing the real world.

Phenotypic plasticity The individual phenotype's capacity to adapt to new circumstances within its lifetime. Individuals of some species can learn during their lifetimes. This is a great advantage over other species which can adapt only across generations, through natural selection.

Physical stance Framework, made explicit by Dennett, for explaining and predicting systems based on information about their physical states and relevant laws of physics. For example, when one explains that one's computer does not work because it lacks a power source.

Prisoner's dilemma Game-theoretic model of strategic decision-making involving multiple agents. It is used to model social as well as biological phenomena. In the prisoner's dilemma, the best outcome involves defecting while one's partners cooperate but, since all agents think this way, all participants end up defecting – the second-to-worst possible outcome for all.

Projectivism A philosophical theory of the nature of colour and other sensory properties. Since no objective properties correspond to our commonsense judgements of colour, the mind must *project* colours onto external objects.

Propositional attitudes Philosophical term for mental states with propositional, or sentential, content. For example, the content of my belief that Washington DC is the capital of the United States is given by the proposition expressed in the sentence, 'Washington DC is the capital of the United States.' My belief is an attitude toward this proposition.

Punctate self Dennett's term for the assumption behind many incompatibilist theories of freedom of the will. For the will to be truly efficacious, it must consist in a concrete, datable, microscopic event in the brain. Dennett is critical of this view.

Qualia Philosophical term for the intrinsic properties of conscious experiences. According to many philosophers, consciousness consists in the subject's qualia. These are intrinsic because experiences with different qualia can have the same cause–effect relations to other states, and experiences with the same qualia can have different cause–effect relations to other states.

Realism Realism about some concept is the view that the concept corresponds to something real in the world. Realism about mental states is the view that there really are mental states. It comes in different strengths: from the strong realism of the language of thought hypothesis (beliefs are mentalese sentences in the brain), to Dennett's 'mild' realism about intentional patterns.

Reductionism A philosophical position on the relation between higher- and lower-level categories. Strong reductionists believe that for a higher-level category, like belief, to be real, it must really be identical to a lower-level category, like brain state or function.

Self-consciousness To be self-conscious is to know that and of what one is conscious while one is conscious of it. Though most agree that many non-human animals are conscious, they show little evidence of self-consciousness.

Serial processing A kind of computation typical of standard desktop computers. One powerful processor processes items of information serially, that is, one at a time.

Skyhook Dennett's term for an appeal to miraculous intervention in explaining natural design. Rather than explaining the emergence of design in terms of blind mechanisms, as cranes do, skyhooks explain the emergence of design by appeal to unexplained intelligence.

Soft determinism A compatibilist position on the problem of freedom of the will. Some human behaviour is both freely chosen and determined at the same time. This is Dennett's position.

Spandrel Stephen Jay Gould's term for a biological trait that is the outcome of architectural constraints on development, rather than selection for an adaptive function. The term is borrowed from architecture: it denotes structures used to hold up cathedral domes, which, according to Gould, are inevitable by-products of mounting a dome on rounded arches, rather than intended architectural designs.

Subjective The way the world appears to a particular, limited perspective. It contrasts with the way the world really is, i.e., the objective nature of the world.

Turing Machine Abstract, mathematical model, proposed by Alan Turing, of a mechanism capable of computing any algorithmically specifiable function. Any problem for which there is, in principle, a step-by-step solution can be solved by a Turing Machine.

Verificationism   A philosophical view according to which, for any claim to be true or false, there must be a method of testing for or verifying it.

Virtual Machine   Term from computer science for special-purpose 'machines' specified by software run on general-purpose computers. For example, word processors are virtual machines specified in terms of software run on the hardware of standard desktop computers.

Von Neumann Machine   Any computer, like standard desktop computers, consisting of a single, powerful processor capable of simple operations on information imported from a reliable and capacious memory, such as the 'hard drive' of most computers.

Zombie   Philosophical term for a hypothetical physical duplicate of a conscious person that lacks consciousness. From the 'outside' zombies are indistinguishable from their conscious counterparts: they undergo the same brain states and produce the same behaviours. However, from the 'inside' they are very different: they lack qualia.

Bibliography

Key books by Dennett are referenced within the text by the following letter codes:

BS   1978. *Brainstorms*. Cambridge, MA, MIT Press.
ER   1984. *Elbow Room*. Cambridge, MA, MIT Press.
IS   1987. *The Intentional Stance*. Cambridge, MA, MIT Press.
CE   1991. *Consciousness Explained*. Boston, Little, Brown and Company.
DDI   1995. *Darwin's Dangerous Idea*. New York, Simon and Schuster.
BC   1998. *Brainchildren*. Cambridge, MA, MIT Press.
FE   2003. *Freedom Evolves*. New York, Viking.
SD   2005. *Sweet Dreams*. Cambridge, MA, MIT Press.

Other works cited

Ainslie, G. 2001. *Breakdown of Will*. Cambridge, UK, Cambridge University Press.
Austin, J. 1961. 'Ifs and Cans', in J. O. Urmson and G. Warnock (eds) *Philosophical Papers*, pp. 205–32. Cambridge, Cambridge University Press.
Block, N. 1993. 'Review of Consciousness Explained', *Journal of Philosophy*, 90, 181–93.
Boesch, C. 1991. 'Teaching among wild chimpanzees', *Animal Behaviour*, 41, 530–32.

Boyd, R. and Richerson, P. 1992. 'Punishment Allows the Evolution of Cooperation (or Anything Else) in Sizable Groups', *Ethology and Sociobiology*, 13, 171–95.

Boyd, R. and Richerson, P. 1996. 'Why Culture is Common, but Cultural Evolution is Rare', *Proceedings of the British Academy*, 88, 77–93.

Chaitin, G. 1975. 'Randomness and Mathematical Proof', *Scientific American*, 232, 47–52.

Chalmers, D. 1996. *The Conscious Mind*. Oxford, Oxford University Press.

Chisholm, R. 1982. 'Human Freedom and the Self', in G. Watson (ed.) *Free Will*, pp. 26–37. Oxford, Oxford University Press.

Churchland, P. M. 1981. 'Eliminative Materialism and the Propositional Attitudes', *Journal of Philosophy*, 78(2), 67–90.

Churchland, P. M. 1982. 'Is "Thinker" a Natural Kind?', *Dialogue*, 21, 223–38.

Churchland, P. M. 1989. *A Neurocomputational Perspective*. Cambridge, MA, MIT Press.

Churchland, P. S. and Ramachandran, V. S. 1993. 'Filling In: Why Dennett is Wrong', in B. Dahlbom (ed.) *Dennett and his Critics*, pp. 28–52. Oxford, Blackwell.

Cronin, H. 1991. *The Ant and the Peacock*. Cambridge, UK, Cambridge University Press.

Davidson, D. 1984. *Inquiries into Truth and Interpretation*. Oxford, Clarendon Press.

Davidson, D. 2001. *Essays on Actions and Events*. Oxford, Clarendon Press.

Darwin, C. 1959. *The Origin of Species by Charles Darwin: A Variorum Text*, ed. M. Peckham. Pittsburgh, PA, University of Pennsylvania Press.

Dawkins, R. 1976. *The Selfish Gene*. Oxford, Oxford University Press.

Dawkins, R. 1982. *The Extended Phenotype*. San Francisco, CA, Freeman.

Dawkins, R. 1986. *The Blind Watchmaker*. London, Longmans.

Dennett, D. 1983. 'Intentional Systems in Cognitive Ethology: the "Panglossian Paradigm" Defended', *Behavioural and Brain Sciences*, 6, 343–90.

Dennett, D. 1988. 'Quining Qualia', in A. Marcel and E. Bisiach (eds) *Consciousness in Contemporary Science*, pp. 42–77. New York, Oxford University Press.

Dennett, D. 1993. 'Back from the Drawing board', in B. Dahlbom (ed.) *Dennett and his Critics*, pp. 203–35. Oxford, Blackwell.

Dennett, D. 2000. 'With a Little Help from my Friends', in D. Ross, A. Brook and D. Thompson (eds) *Dennett's Philosophy*, pp. 327–88. Cambridge, MA, MIT Press.

Dennett, D. 2006. *Breaking the Spell: Religion as a Natural Phenomenon.* New York, Viking Adult.

Dennett, D. and Kinsbourne, M. 1992. 'Time and the Observer: the Where and When of Consciousness in the Brain', *Behavioural and Brain Sciences*, 15, 183–247.

Descartes, R. 1984. *Meditations on First Philosophy*, in J. Cottingham, R. Stoothoff and D. Murdoch (trans./eds) *The Philosophical Writings of Descartes*, volume II, pp. 1–62. Cambridge, UK, Cambridge University Press.

Eigen, M. 1992. *Steps towards Life.* Oxford, Oxford University Press.

Fodor, J. 1975. *The Language of Thought.* Cambridge, MA, Harvard University Press.

Fodor, J. 1987. *Psychosemantics.* Cambridge, MA, MIT Press.

Fodor, J. and Lepore, E. 1993. 'Is Intentional Ascription Intrinsically Normative?', in B. Dahlbom (ed.) *Dennett and his Critics*, pp. 70–82. Oxford, Blackwell.

Frank, R. H. 1988. *Passions within Reason: The Strategic Role of the Emotions.* New York, Norton.

Gould, S. J. and Eldredge, N. 1993. 'Punctuated Equilibrium Comes of Age', *Nature*, 366, 223–7.

Gould, S. J. and Lewontin, R. 1979. 'The Spandrels of San Marco and the Panglossian Paradigm: A Critique of the Adaptationist Programme', *Proceedings of the Royal Society*, B205, 581–98.

Gould, S. J. and Vrba, E. 1981. 'Exaptation: A Missing Term in the Science of Form', *Paleobiology*, 8, 4–15.

Hamilton, W. 1964. 'The Genetical Evolution of Social Behaviour, pts. I and II', *Journal of Theoretical Biology*, 7, 1–52.

Hardcastle, V. 1998. 'The Binding Problem', in W. Bechtel and G. Graham (eds) *A Companion to Cognitive Science*, pp. 555–65. Oxford, Blackwell.

Husserl, E. 1982. *Ideas Pertaining to a Pure Phenomenology and to a Phenomenological Philosophy – First Book: General Introduction to a Pure Phenomenology.* The Hague, Nijhoff.

Jackson, F. 1982. 'Epiphenomenal Qualia', *Philosophical Quarterly*, 32 (127), 127–36.

Kane, R. 1996. *The Significance of Free Will.* Oxford, Oxford University Press.

Kipling, R. 1912. *Just So Stories.* Garden City, NY, Doubleday.

Küppers, B. 1990. *Information and the Origin of Life*. Cambridge, MA, MIT Press.

Levine, J. 1983. 'Materialism and Qualia', *Pacific Philosophical Quarterly*, 64, 354–61.

Libet, B. 1999. 'Do We Have Free Will?', in B. Libet *et al.* (eds) *The Volitional Brain: Towards a Neuroscience of Free Will*, pp. 47–58. Thorverton, UK, Imprint Academic.

Liebniz, G. 1989. 'The Monadology', in R. Ariew and D. Garber (trans./eds) *Philosophical Essays*, pp. 213–25. Indianapolis, IN, Hackett Publishing Company.

Marr, D. 1982. *Vision*. San Francisco, CA, W. H. Freeman.

McGinn, C. 1999. 'Can We Solve the Mind-Body Problem?', *Mind*, 98, 349–66.

Minsky, M. 1985. *The Society of Mind*. New York, Simon and Schuster.

Nagel, T. 1974. 'What Is It Like to Be a Bat?', *Philosophical Review*, 83 (4), 435–50.

Putnam, H. 1960. 'Minds and Machines', in S. Hook (ed.) *Dimensions of Mind*, pp. 138–64. New York, New York University Press.

Quine, W. 1960. *Word and Object*. Cambridge, MA, MIT Press.

Ramsey, W., Stich, S. and Garon, J. 1995. 'Connectionism, Eliminativism, and the Future of Folk Psychology', in C. MacDonald (ed.) *Connectionism: Debates on Psychological Explanation*, pp. 199–225. Cambridge, MA, Blackwell.

Rorty, R. 1993. 'Holism, Intrinsicality, and the Ambition of Transcendence', in B. Dahlbom (ed.) *Dennett and his Critics*, pp. 184–202. Oxford, Blackwell.

Ross, D. 2000. 'Introduction: The Dennettian Stance', in D. Ross, A. Brook and D. Thompson (eds) *Dennett's Philosophy*, pp. 1–26. Cambridge, MA, MIT Press.

Rumelhart, D. E., McClelland, J. L. and the PDP Research Group (eds) 1986. *Parallel Distributed Processing*. Cambridge, MA, MIT Press.

Ryle, G. 1949. *The Concept of Mind*. London, Penguin Books.

Searle, J. 1995. 'Review of *Consciousness Explained*', *The New York Review of Books*, 42 (November 16), 56–9.

Sellars, W. 1956. 'Empiricism and Philosophy of Mind', in H. Feigl and M. Scriven (eds) *Minnesota Studies in the Philosophy of Science, vol. I: The Foundations of Science and the Concepts of Psychology and Psychoanalysis*, pp. 253–329.

Sellars, W. 1963. *Science, Perception and Reality*. London, Routledge and Kegan Paul.

Stich, S. 1982. 'Dennett on Intentional Systems', in J. I. Biro and R. W. Shahan (eds) *Mind, Brain, and Function*, pp. 39–62. Norman, OK, University of Oklahoma Press.

Stich, S. 1983. *From Folk Psychology to Cognitive Science*. Cambridge, MA, MIT Press.

Strawson, G. 1992. 'Review of *Consciousness Explained*', *Times Literary Supplement*, 4664 (August 21), 5–6.

Strawson, G. 2003. 'Review of *Freedom Evolves*', *New York Times Book Review*, 108(9), 11.

Titchener, E. 1898. *A Primer of Psychology*. New York, Macmillan.

Tittle, P. 2005. *What If...* New York, Pearson.

Tomasello, M., Kruger, A. C. and Ratner, H. H. 1993. 'Cultural learning', *Behavioural and Brain Sciences*, 16, 495–52.

Wason, P. C. 1960. 'On the failure to eliminate hypotheses in a conceptual task', *Quarterly Journal of Experimental Psychology*, 12, 129–40.

White, S. L. 1991. *The Unity of the Self*. Cambridge, MA, MIT Press.

Wittgenstein, L. 1953. *Philosophical Investigations*. Oxford, Blackwell.

Index